Dedicated to Our Blessed Mother

Dear Fr. Kevin,

Thanks for the many many ways you have supported homeschoolers over the years. I have no doubt that you are part of the triumph of Mary's Heart.

L. Michell

THE GIFT AND GRACE OF HOMESCHOOLING

A Gift to Homeschooling Mothers

The Gift and Grace of Homeschooling: A Gift to Homeschooling Mothers
by Michelle Heekin
Edited by Patt Allen

hope you enjoy!
-Mary Grace 24

Cover artwork by Mary Grace Heekin
Cover design by Fiverr
Interior layout and formatting by Bret Thoman

Copyright © by Michelle Heekin. 2021
All rights reserved.
ISBN: 978-0-578-97396-8

Upon this rock I will build my church and the gates of hell will not prevail against it.

Matthew 16:18

THE ROAD NOT TAKEN
BY ROBERT FROST

Two roads diverged in a yellow wood,
And sorry I could not travel both
And be one traveler, long I stood
And looked down one as far as I could
To where it bent in the undergrowth;

Then took the other, as just as fair,
And having perhaps the better claim,
Because it was grassy and wanted wear;
Though as for that the passing there
Had worn them really about the same,

And both that morning equally lay
In leaves no step had trodden black.
Oh, I kept the first for another day!
Yet knowing how way leads on to way,
I doubted if I should ever come back.

I shall be telling this with a sigh
Somewhere ages and ages hence:
Two roads diverged in a wood, and I—
I took the one less traveled by,
And that has made all the difference.

Contents

Acknowledgements

In gratitude and appreciation, I wish to acknowledge the following souls, who have contributed to the completion of this work.

My "St. Joseph" of 25 years, Chris Heekin, whose love and support has carried me through many storms with a lighthearted breeze. He made this work possible with his unfailing support.

Our family, beginning with our oldest son, "St. Michael," whose birth first heralded that I was to be a mother, and whose humor and warmth never fails to brighten a room.

Our "lady-bug," Mary Grace, who has just the right touch in every situation, whether the right scientific terminology, perfect piece of art, or baking extravagance. Everything she does is with excellence and love. It is her work which graces the book's cover.

The "grandmaster" of the family, John, whose logic and wit have been as sharpened iron in my writing and homeschooling.

Our little "explosive rhino," Christopher, whose contagious and joyful heart never fails to propel me forward, along the right path.

Cheryl Roch, my own mother, who is simply the best mother living on the earth. She has taught me so much of patience, of wisdom, of love, and of how to follow the simple, loving path.

Adrienne Heekin, my dear mother-in-law, who showed me the grace of mothering. She is as elegant and graceful a mother, as I have ever known. She is a lady of grace.

Linda Smith, a spiritual mother to me. One cannot look at her face and not see the Blessed Mother.

Patt Allen, the book's editor, an experienced wordsmith and a veteran homeschool Mom herself. Her calmness and joy gave me the courage to continue this dual (homeschooling and writing) journey on more occasions than I can count.

Father Kevin who has supported the local homeschooling group. All grow taller in his vibrant presence. His humor and wit have kept our children engaged and entertained, as well.

Father Martin, LC who has blessed so many with his gift of counsel and priestly vocation.

Cricket Aull, Laura Berquist, Bret Thoman, The Sisters of Life and Matthew Kelly whose writing has inspired me. I am hopeful that I stand on the shoulders of your writing in some way.

To my dear friends Aileen Malneritch, Tracy Sands, Kelly Carney, Shalene Frisch and Debby Guisti, who have so encouraged me. You have been my cheerleaders in this work.

AUTHOR'S NOTE

The Dear Friend in Christ:

This book is written out of a love for those on the homeschool journey and out of a love for the Church.

For those moms on the homeschool journey, my heart is for you. My hope is to be your cheerleader, as you shape your children's hearts, souls and minds in Christ. The work that you are doing is sacred and will move mountains in the future. Be not afraid.

For the Church, I believe that homeschooling families and communities bring special blessings to their individual parishes and congregations. And there are now many, many successful homeschooling mothers. This ever-expanding educational choice is filled with so much hope and creativity.

My prayer for this book is that it will fulfill the Holy Father Francis' request that the laity come forward with energy, inspiration, and vision to help make the Church strong and holy; to help it become the Church the Lord desires. Pope Francis addressed the Church, saying, "We need lay people who take risks, who get their hands dirty, who are not afraid of making mistakes, who go forward. We need lay people with a vision of the future...." (June 18, 2016, Plenary Assembly of the Pontifical Council for the Laity).

Although this book is written primarily for Catholic homeschool mothers, it may well be picked up by others, and I want it to be a blessing (in some way) for all who are led to read it!

For fathers: I admire and respect you. I am so very thankful for your support and encouragement, most especially for my own dear husband. Parts of this book may serve as confirmation of your family's decision to homeschool. I pray that you will have abundant peace in your family and continued direction from the Lord. May you walk with the Lord in all you do.

For all mothers: Much of what is written can be applied to a variety of mothering situations, even if one is not homeschooling – and I encourage you to apply what is helpful. My prayer for all mothers is that you are blessed with the grace of drawing near to the Blessed Mother and that you be grafted into her heart.

For Christians: I am so thankful for your presence in my life. I have been blessed to cross paths, especially as a homeschool Mom, with believers from various Christian denominations, and I have found Christ alive in your hearts and in your lives. What a gift you are to the world. I pray that we may continue to draw together in unity. May we also persist in sharing the message of Christ's love to a world that is so in need of our God-given hope at this time.

For those who are not homeschooling: Jesus's words and actions lead us closer to Him in love. Love is the path… not necessarily (or always) homeschooling. May you be blessed to grow in the knowledge and love of God.

For those who are theologians: I admire your gift and study of the triune God, as expressed through Church history, teaching and Sacred Scripture. I look to you for insights. I, myself, am not a theologian, a saint, or a mystic. So if my theology seems off at times … it may be. It is hard to know sometimes where God stops, and I, the humble homeschool mother begin. But I do believe that some of what I have written will bless others, and so I share my thoughts as a gift to the Church. I pray it may inspire you, as you study and write and continue to serve the Lord.

Finally, I have taken a few liberties in my writing by presenting the ideal or optimum family homeschool situation – while seeming to ignore the daunting realities of everyday family life. So, let me acknowledge some of those here:

1) I may seem to present homeschooling as a neat, quiet, peaceful, heavenly activity. Ha, ha! Homeschooling is messy... very messy ... you are working with children.... And you are working with children's formation. It is muddy, and that is the truth.

And, yes, the world I describe is a bit idealistic. I have done this on purpose, so that when we have finished fighting a battle or successfully overcoming a particular challenge – and life feels a bit "out of shape" – we have a clear picture of the "ideal," as we seek to return to "normal." It's hard to attain "normal" in its best sense, if we don't know what it should look like.

Regarding the various suggestions/systems or ideas found in these pages, it is my hope that as you read, one or two lights will shine brightly, and that you will have a few "Aha!" moments that will inspire you; and, that eventually you will try selected new or improved ways of leading and teaching your children. The goal is not to push you to adopt a new vision or implement a new system, but to offer food for thought, encouragement, and ideas.

2) As a loving Mom, I might be tempted to portray our family as a bit saintly. Again, "Ha ha!" We are a rough-and-tumble family with plenty of energy. But I chose not to emphasize those jagged edges, because I, personally, am more inspired by hearing or reading about what actually works. I hope to be a positive resource in this discussion of homeschooling, rather than dwell on any negatives. I made the assumption that you would feel the same way. But if you need to know what my family is like, I assure you, it is normal, just like yours!

And with that... let us take a step forward ... and begin our journey together.

1: Hope for the Homeschooling Mother

Dear Homeschool Mom:

This is a time of grace for you and for all homeschooling mothers. I hope that you will enter into this time with enthusiasm and with great joy. In many ways "it is your time."

Hope Has Arrived

In 1917, Our Lady appeared in Fatima calling the world to conversion, prayer, and penance with an amazing promise just for you, saying **"My Immaculate Heart will triumph."**

I have no doubt that a part of this Triumph of Mary's Immaculate Heart will be through the gift and grace of homeschooling – grace that is being poured into your Heart. Mary is sharing her heart with you and with millions of your closest friends, other homeschooling mothers across the world. In addition, she is using you and your example to shape and mold the Church. She is sharing her maternal heart with the Church through your example and inspiration. You have an incredible calling, and light shines brightly in your heart.

Our Blessed Mother walks so closely with you and is the light our heavenly Father is sending the Church during this time. Our heavenly Mother and her presence is found walking upon the earth in the presence of mothers.... And is to be found especially in your heart as a homeschool mom.

I believe through your decision to homeschool, that she is pouring into your heart her very own, and an abundance of, traditions, and teachings, to pass along to your children... the very best of the best. I believe you are being called to focus on your child(ren) and to fulfill your vocation as a mother. And through your efforts, this gift of wisdom can be poured out for the Church.

A New Time

Saint Pope John Paul II prophesied that there would be a new evangelization. We have seen such spreading of the Church to reach so many with the Gospel. It is a time of zeal for the faith. Radio stations are popping up, the web offers countless online Gospel reflections, and printed literature abounds. EWTN continues to reach around the globe, and numerous evangelists travel both physically, and through online resources, sharing the Gospel message of salvation.

But what if the New Evangelization, alongside this zealous outreach, had a specific mission for you... and included a NEWNESS... a NEW way of doing things...a way to a deeper holiness and imitation of Christ as He grew His little flock of disciples.... A new way of growing the domestic church in DEPTH, in relationship, which could be passed on to the larger Church?

What if the emphasis in the words NEW EVANGELIZATION, was on the word NEW as much as evangelization?

What if the new systems to implement, included homeschooling models, as a significant piece of this new evangelization, of this new growth?

What if the growth ALSO consisted in growing DEEP as well as growing wide? What if these new methods allowed the Church to live the call "they will know we are Christians by our love" a bit more fully, so that all could see it?

What if your very own homeschooling family could aid in bringing this newness to fruition by your example, and models and mindset that you already have in place?

What if by your homeschooling example and wisdom which God has placed in your heart, you could aid the Church in fulfilling her two-fold mission of "to preach the Gospel and lead all people to holiness." (Note: *Following Christ, Faith and Life Series Grade 6* (Ignatius Press 2005).

What if, by your faithfulness in your response to the call to homeschool your children **you are actually part of the "triumph of Mary's Immaculate Heart"?**

In some way I believe that your call to homeschooling and this homeschooling movement has the potential to do just that. It has the potential to "spring forward" your efforts as a mother. It also has the potential to form your child(ren) in holiness as you educate them; through your focus, your heart, and your courageous direction, this grace of homeschooling can powerfully minister to and even evangelize the larger Church.

That is no small call for you, being a Homeschooling mom… that is a mission, and that is hope. I pray this encourages you as a mother and for the Church you love.

God Bless,
Michelle

2: What is Homeschooling?

Dear Homeschooling Mom:

As we begin our journey together, let us first examine and define what homeschooling is; and the best way to do that is to say what homeschooling is not.

What Homeschooling is NOT:
Homeschooling is not a belief that there is only one way to educate a child… from home. We often encounter in our lives "a push/ pressure" to embrace one movement or another – or one way of doing things as the best vs. another. You know as well as do I that there is simply not a "best way" to educate all children across the board.

We can reflect upon canonized saints of traditional schools. Saint Elizabeth Ann Seton established an entire chain of traditional schools, and through her efforts, the virtue and formation of the Catholic faith flourished throughout the United States. I have no doubt that traditional schools are continuing to grow students in virtue and will bear wonderful fruit for the future.

Homeschooling is not a belief.

Homeschooling is also not a cut-and-paste fit for every child. Your child's/children's hearts and spirits are unique; where one child thrives, another may not. Our society is full of factories which produce millions of identical products, and similarly, there can be a tendency to follow one course of direction for every child, expecting to get the same results. From experience, any veteran homeschooling mother will tell you that results vary and are dependent upon many factors. Thus, it is of paramount importance to listen to the Lord's voice and guidance, as you pray about the best way to educate each of your children.

Homeschooling is not a factory or program with guaranteed results. Sorry....

Homeschooling is not a threat to traditional schools. There is a sense among some that homeschooling families are "taking away" students and funding from traditional Catholic schools. To counter these fears, we stand firm and remember that holiness and truth always attract. Traditional schools founded in virtue and truth will only continue to thrive as more and more families seek authentic and righteous education for their children. These schools need our support, prayers, and encouragement to continue the holy work they are accomplishing.

The call to attend a traditional school is different than the call to homeschool. From experience, I can tell you that sooner or later (either with the child or the parent), inauthentic actions come to light. A child who needs to be homeschooled, but who is being educated in a traditional school, will sooner or later experience a sense of unease, a lack of peace. And similarly, a homeschooled child who would better grow and thrive in a traditional school will eventually grow restless, and the parent will sense in this a lack of peace in his/her own heart, as well.

Homeschooling is not a threat.

Homeschooling is finally not a system to be compulsorily enforced or implemented by a group of people. Like everything else, homeschooling requires balance and discernment. It interweaves a number of systems or gears which should naturally fit into place. It should be surrounded by a sense of abiding peace, although there may be conflicts from others or doubts from self. There should be a sense of direction, rightness, and order.

Homeschooling is not a cult.

A Simple Definition

Simply put, I believe that homeschooling is a call within a call. This inner call is to educate one's children, and it is fulfilled as the parents are used by God as instruments of formation. The setting – the location for this education and formation – is the family home with support from a homeschooling community.

The Outer Call

On the altar, a husband and wife make three promises as they commit their lives to each other. One of these promises is "to raise any children they are blessed with in the Catholic Faith." This promise is so important that the Church insists upon it as part of a valid Sacrament of Marriage, and it is usually made before God, in front of His altar. This is the call of Marriage life.

This outer call is most clearly seen in the words of the Declaration of Christian Education, in which the Church says: "Since parents have given children their life, they are bound by the most serious obligation to educate their offspring and therefore must be recognized as the primary and principal educators." The education/formation of children is the duty and responsibility of parents.

The Inner Call

The call within the call is to fulfill this formation and education by living this promise in fullness by being the instrument of teaching to fulfill this vow.

In homeschooling, so many graces are abundantly poured into a mother's heart for her child. Her soul overflows with wisdom and joy in teaching, with insights and discoveries, and with love of all that God created – so much so, that she cannot help but pass these riches on to her children through instruction. She sees the beauty of these graces and willingly sacrifices much to bestow all this on her child(ren) through sharing her own heart.

At Home

The home is the center and primary location of formation and education, where the parent(s) – usually the mother – shares deeply from the heart. A mother can be considered the heart of the home, and homeschooling emerges from her heart.

Homeschooling is especially a grace given/bestowed upon families during times of trial… perhaps the result of a family member's illness or frequent or untimely moves. It also can be a special grace, as families embrace their special needs child, or when the traditional (or available) school setting is not a good fit for one reason or another. It is also a gift to large families, who can easily become overwhelmed by children in too many classrooms and schools with multiple teachers, locations, activities, and sports to juggle. Homeschooling then is able to provide more of a center to the whole family. Also, it is a grace especially given when children need to be protected from society or the prevailing culture.

Perhaps the tremendous grace given to the Church in recent years reflects the last situation, where many schools and media are filled with temptation, impulsivity, and quite honestly, sin. Social media alone would fit into this category. Children's souls are being exposed to images they are unprepared to process. Simply, the loss of innocence is at stake.

In Community

From experience, homeschooling families often (but not always) journey together and come together to form a community, a little "school" if you will. Each family takes one role or another in a co-op/hybrid academy, and the children form friendships that last for years. This is a beautiful movement of the Holy Spirit to behold, as children are excited to join together for Mass, celebration of feast days, field trips, and educational endeavors. One of the reasons homeschooling communities are so beautiful lies in the fact that they are generally small and intimate, and each child therein is known and understood.

As you consider homeschooling, may He fill the vessel of your heart to overflowing bringing light, and wisdom to your children.

God Bless,
Michelle

3: Traditional Roots of Homeschooling

Dear Homeschool Mom:

Any tree that grows tall also must grow "deep." In order to grow deep in the "grace of homeschooling," it is wise to look at the traditional roots. Thus, I would like to spend some time with you, considering those early beginnings – a foundation that many homeschooling mothers have reflected upon or wondered about. The best place to start this journey is my favorite place – with our Blessed Mother.

Pondering Mary's Early Life

Tradition tells us, although we most likely will never know for sure, that during her young years the Blessed Mother journeyed with her parents to the temple where she was presented as a beautiful virgin – and where she remained during her youth. Although this most likely broke her parents' heart, and caused Mary natural sadness, I believe Mary's heart soared at the thought of being so close to the Lord's temple. I picture her walking up flights of wide stairs, taking several steps up, then turning back to her parents with a little wave, and eventually running wholeheartedly up the remaining terraced flights – to the temple and elders. She gave herself (unreservedly) to God, and this is a wonderful thought to ponder in prayer.

In the Temple

In the temple, I see Mary filling her days with prayer before the Holy of Holies (maybe in the outer room of prayer for women). She devoted herself to glorifying the Lord by meditating on the Psalms, learning to pray with the heart, studying the history of Israel, and following the traditions of her people. Was not her focus on the Ark (that was removed and hidden at that time), and on the sacred elements within the Holy of Holies – the Ten Commandments, the rod of Aaron and manna? Did she not consider how this tabernacle was built... with pure gold and Acacia wood . . . of great purity and at great expense, with beautiful designs created by master craftsmen, with every attention to detail? Wasn't it crafted with dedication, precision, and expertise? Did she not consider how the Ark glorified/magnified the objects within, giving them special honor?

In her contemplations, did she not consider how the presence of the Lord dwelt upon this tabernacle resting on the mercy seat? Did she not ponder how the Ark provided a resting place, for this presence, God's presence, to dwell with a seat of gold and angels surrounding... a little heaven... a little home...if you will, created by human hands? In these moments did the Lord not speak to our Blessed Mother's heart, teaching her Himself and demonstrating how a soul could be a resting/dwelling place for Him? Was He not preparing her for her future mission as the new Ark?

Perhaps she pondered how she could be an ark. A vessel of purity and grace to give glory to the Lord and to love others. Perhaps her heart wanted to serve the Lord, to honor Him in every way, His humility, His patience.

Could it not be argued that God Himself taught her, in fact "homeschooled" her as a "Father," her Father in prayer – with abundant knowledge of Himself – teaching as the omniscient, all knowing Father God, and as a tender, loving, personal father? How could she have received her knowledge, or understanding of how to become the mother of our Lord Jesus Christ, but from the eternal Father? Did the holy wisdom to parent God Himself, not come from the Heart of God the Father?

The Ark is Created

Scripture tells us that some years later Mary became betrothed to Joseph, and by the power of the Holy Spirit conceived Jesus the Christ in her womb. In response, she proclaimed "My soul proclaims the greatness of the Lord" (Luke 1: 46) Her every thought, word, and action, would give glory and honor to the presence of the Christ child, protected in her womb . . . and the promises of God the Father, that she pondered in her heart.

Elizabeth, her relative, upon receiving Mary into her home was the first to exclaim, "Blessed are you among women, and blessed is the fruit of your womb" (Luke 1:42).

We can ponder the words of Mary in the Magnificat:

> My soul proclaims the greatness of the Lord; and my spirit rejoices in God my savior. For he has looked upon his handmaid's lowliness; behold, from now on will all ages call me blessed. The Mighty One has done great things for me, and holy is his name. His mercy is from age to age to those who fear him. He has shown might with his arm, dispersed the arrogant of mind and heart. He has thrown down the rulers from their thrones but lifted up the lowly. The hungry he has filled with good things; the rich he has sent away empty. He has helped Israel his servant, remembering his mercy according to his promise to

our fathers, to Abraham and to his descendants forever. (Luke 1:46-55)

Jesus was coming into her womb, and she knew exactly what to do. It was not with gold that Mary built "her ark," but with her love, prayers, reflections, and devotion. Just as Noah built an ark by following the instructions and direction of the Lord, and Moses created the Ark of the Covenant, so, too, Mary cooperated with God in creating the New Ark . . . a resting place, a "Mercy seat," a home, a refuge for the Savior. She was attentive to every detail as were Noah and Moses, and crafted spiritually what her body was growing into physically – a home and a haven.

Focus on Mission

Journeying forward, we find joy in the Nativity, remembering how our Blessed Mother, with Joseph, journeyed to Bethlehem where she gave birth to Jesus. And this was only the beginning of their family travels and trials – we know from Scripture that the Holy Family fled to Egypt and later journeyed to Nazareth. She fled "immediately" at the leading of Saint Joseph, though Mary and Joseph could have attempted to warn the inhabitants or other mothers of Bethlehem.

Mary and Joseph remained totally focused on fulfilling the mission entrusted to them, namely caring for the infant Jesus. This mission was not one of outreach, but of caring for their little domestic church.

Homeschooling Jesus?

In Nazareth (although we have no record) tradition tells us that Mary taught Jesus herself – in essence, schooled Him at home, presumably giving Him a wellspring upon which to draw. We see Jesus at the age of 12, "in the temple, sitting in the midst of the teachers, listening to them and asking them questions" (Luke 2:46). The passage continues, "and all who heard him were astounded at his understanding and his answers" (Luke 2:47).

We have no record that Jesus attended school, but we know that He was well-versed in Scripture and tradition. If Mary indeed was educated in the temple, as such, she would have had exposure to the best teachers in the law, Torah, Psalms, and Old Testament. She would have been filled with abundant knowledge and a heart of prayer. In other words, she would have been more than adequately prepared to teach Jesus. And we certainly know from Scripture that He was more than well-versed in Scripture and wisdom. But this is Jesus's hidden life, and we do not know many details.

I encourage you, as a homeschool mother, to reflect upon Mary's early life – even drawing on accounts of visions from saints and mystics, as you are led by the Holy Spirit. I encourage you to grow to love your Blessed Mother and her early life. Meditating on our blessed Mother's role as the Mother of God will only serve to inspire you in your own motherhood and bless your homeschooling with a richer, deeper grace.

God bless,
Michelle

4: Encouragement through Scripture

Dear Homeschooling Mom:

As we journey through Scripture, we grow in our knowledge and love of God the Father and His only Son, Jesus. I find in Holy Scripture so much wisdom that can be applied to my own homeschooling journey,; and I would like to share with you some key Bible verses and passages that I have reflected upon over the years.

This chapter is presented a bit like a devotional with key scriptures, selected and presented, for your meditation and reflection as you fulfill your role as a homeschool mother. I pray that these treasures from the Word of God may serve as light for your journey.

Creation of Heaven and Earth

We can learn a bit about the Father's Heart in His creation of an earthly home in the story of Creation:

In the beginning, when God created the heavens and the earth, and the earth was without form or shape, with darkness over the abyss and a mighty wind sweeping over the waters- Then God said: "Let there be light," and there was light. God saw that the light was good. God then separated the light from the darkness. God called the light "day," and the darkness he called "night." How good the light was. Evening came, and morning followed-the first day. Then God said: Let there be a dome in the middle of the waters, to separate one body of water from the other. God made the dome, and it separated the water below the dome from the water above the dome. And so it happened. God called the dome "sky." Evening come, and morning followed-the second day. [...] God created mankind in his image, in the image of God he created them; male and female he created them. (Genesis 1:1-8;27)

Through creation, we learn a couple of truths. First, God the Father is a God of order. He ordered the six days of creation, each one building upon the wonders of the previous day(s). He willed that there be a reflection, a magnification of the grace of one day in the creation of the following days. For example, He began with light, separating light from darkness; on the fourth day, He made the stars in the sky.

Second, we learn the joy in creation: "and God looked at everything He had created and found it very good" (Genesis 1:31). God took great joy in seeing the beauty that He created, and He rejoiced in this beauty. Joy is a natural and necessary element of creation.

Creation brings joy. As the homeschooling family creates a family home, this too brings joy – and this joy, like God the Father's joy, is contagious. It leads others to desire to create a "living" home, as well, in their own way and in their own time.

But most importantly, everything God the Father did told of His great love for mankind. Everything was perfectly placed, so that His children could discover and ponder great secrets, untold mysteries, and boundless beauty – all leading us closer to God. It was for man that water and trees, animals and all of life were formed. Adam and Eve dwelt in the world – specifically the garden – that God created. The stars, the majestic sun, the radiant moon, night and day – all were created for man to ponder the infinite nature of God.

In homeschooling, we also have the opportunity to create a world in which our children can thrive and grow closer to God. The books, people, environment, and community we place around them should all lead them closer to Jesus. We are creating an environment in which our child(ren) can flourish. And because this is a creative process, this flourishing often brings much JOY.

I encourage you as a homeschool mother, to create (to your heart's content) a nurturing and living environment for your child(ren). When you do so, you wisely imitate the actions of the Almighty, as you create beauty, harmony, and a living family culture. This brings God, your Father, great joy, as you imitate Him and draw close to him.

Flight into Egypt

One of the first scenes of the Holy Family after the birth of Jesus is found in the biblical narrative of "an angel of the Lord" directing Joseph to flee into Egypt: "Rise, take the child and his mother, flee to Egypt, and stay there until I tell you. Joseph rose and took the child and his mother by night and departed for Egypt" (Matthew 2:13-14).

We can glean a couple of lessons from the Holy Family's example pertaining to homeschooling. First, their focus was on their child. They left the "world" in a sense – their neighbors, friends, and even culture – and journeyed by themselves into the land of Egypt. We also learn about the focus of Joseph and Mary. Their haste seems to indicate a sense of impending danger, but their focus is on fulfilling the angel's wishes – the protection and care of the infant Jesus. While we do not know for sure, it does not ring true that

Joseph or Mary began to tell others about the dream or the looming peril. They were focused on shielding and lovingly tending to their little Jesus. This was their apostolate, their "call" in life, and they fulfilled it beautifully. In a certain sense, because of their care of Jesus and their obedience to the angel's direction, we have Jesus as our Savior.

As a homeschooling mother, have no fear about choosing your "little flock" as your primary apostolate. Know that you are planting seeds which will bear fruit in the future.

Young Jesus in the Temple

Up until this time, until this moment in history, God was seen as an almighty power, a lord, a master. Only to King David does the Lord say, "I shall be like a "Father to you" (2 Samuel 7:14).

In the temple, with one powerful sentence Jesus proclaims the truth about the first Person of the Holy Trinity, God the Father. "Did you not know that I must be in my FATHER'S house?" (Luke 2:49).

In that one simple question, Jesus's first recorded words, we receive an entire revelation about God as Father and Jesus as a Son of His Father: in MY Father's house. In a sense, Jesus's entire mission is proclaimed in this verse – a revelation of God the Father in the person of Jesus, as well as a deeper understanding of the relationship between the Father and the Son.

Let us examine Jesus's response further. Jesus is among "teachers" in "his Father's house." Scripture does not say among elders, but among TEACHERS. We learn two things from this: first, that His Father's house is filled with teaching; and second, that the place where His Father is, Jesus refers to as "house." Jesus does not say business or place. The house is a dwelling place full of teaching. Could heaven be imagined any other way… a home filled with the loving continued instruction/revelation from the Father? It's just a thought to ponder, but it would fulfill the verse: "They shall all be taught by God" (John 6:45).

I encourage you also to contemplate the example of Jesus in *proclaiming* His Father. He does so unabashedly, courageously, and with great love. He walks into His mission, and I believe as He does so, He encourages you to walk into yours.

Instructing the Disciples

Journeying forward with Jesus, we continually see this pattern of instruction and leading by example. Jesus does not send His disciples "away" to learn from another teacher. Instead, He frequently draws this "unschooled" group around Him and teaches them truths about Himself. He takes the time, sees His disciples as children, and instructs them Himself.

Let us ponder Matthew 13 and the parable of sowing seeds:

> On that day, Jesus went out of the house and sat down by the sea. Such large crowds gathered around him that he got into a boat and sat down, and the whole crowd stood along the shore. And he spoke to them at length in parables, saying: "A sower went out to sow. And as he sowed, some seed fell on the path, and birds came and ate it up. Some fell on rocky ground, where it had little soil. It sprang up at once because the soil was not deep, and when the sun rose it was scorched, and it withered for lack of roots. Some seed fell among thorns, and the thorns grew up and choked it. But some seed fell on rich soil, and produced fruit, a hundred or sixty or thirtyfold. Whoever has ears ought to hear." (1-9)

The disciples approached him and said, "Why do you speak to them in parables?" He said to them in reply, "Because knowledge of the mysteries of the kingdom of heaven has been granted to you, but to them it has not been granted. To anyone who has, more will be given, and he will grow rich; from anyone who has not, even what he has will be taken away. This is why I speak to them in parables, because 'they look but do not see and hear but do not listen or understand." (10-13)

Isaiah's prophecy is fulfilled in them, which says: "You shall indeed hear but not understand, you shall indeed look but never see. Gross is the heart of this people, they will hardly hear with their ears, they have closed their eyes, lest they see with their eyes and hear with their ears and understand with their heart and be converted, and I heal them." (14-15)

But blessed are your eyes, because they see, and your ears, because they hear. Amen, I say to you, many prophets and righteous people longed to see what you see but did not see it, and to hear what you hear but did not hear it (16-17).

Hear then the parable of the sower. The seed sown on the path is the one who hears the word of the kingdom without understanding it, and the evil one comes and steals away what was sown in his heart. The seed sown on rocky ground is the one who hears the word and receives it at once with joy. But he has no root and lasts only for a time. When some tribulation or persecution comes because of the word, he immediately falls away. The seed sown among thorns is the one who hears the word, but then worldly anxiety and the lure of riches choke the word and it bears no fruit. But the seed sown on rich soil is the one who hears the word and understands it, who indeed bears fruit and yields a hundred or sixty or thirtyfold (18-23).

Jesus shared the parable with the crowds, and gave a deeper understanding to the disciples, those privileged to be closest to Him; He shared His very Heart and a very deep understanding. He "homeschooled" them, in a sense, as little children, thereby enlightening them about spiritual truths. This understanding is born not out of a religious mindset, but comes to life through the relationship Jesus has with them.

What did Jesus's disciples gain from His words in the passages quoted above? Consider the depth of meaning in verses 16-17, "But blessed are your eyes, because they see . . . many prophets and righteous people longed to see what you see, but did not see it . . ." He, Jesus, in essence draws a circle around them, as His chosen ones, privileged to see and hear what the servants of old never saw or heard. And, through this understanding, their hearts are drawn and connected to Jesus in a special way that the crowds cannot comprehend.

They received a greater understanding of the parable and its spiritual truths. "But the seed sown on rich soil is the one who hears the word and understands it." Their questions were answered personally, and their desire for a deeper understanding was granted. "Because knowledge of the kingdom of God has been granted to you... To anyone who has, more will be given..." (Matthew 13:11-12). Can we not apply the same grace, understanding, and wisdom as we homeschool those whom God has entrusted to us, our own precious children?

We also should reflect upon the primacy of relationship, as Jesus taught and walked with His disciples. He drew these young men especially close to Him to allow them to really know Him and hear His Heart. He even gave his disciples a commandment to "love one another as I have loved you" (John 15:12). This differs from the instruction He gave to the crowds to "love your neighbor as yourself." His commandment to His disciples is stronger, and, yes, filled with greater promise and challenge. His words are clear and speak to the formation of a family, which later becomes the apostolic foundation of the Church.

I encourage you to ponder the gift of time in developing a strong relationship with your children. This time is precious. Use it wisely, and do not allow yourself to be distracted from the blessing at hand. The gift of following in the footsteps of your Lord and Savior and instructing your disciple(s) is priceless. I encourage you to savor it and not to doubt the potential and eternal value of the seeds you are planting today.

And Who is My Mother?

While growing up, I remember desiring so much to be "Mary" in the Christmas play each year, or to crown Mary on Mother's Day. Perhaps you felt the same way. It is such an honor to be close to the Blessed Mother. Jesus recognizes even this desire to be close to our Blessed Mother among His disciples with His teaching:

> While he was still speaking to the crowd, his mother and his brothers appeared outside, wishing to speak with him. (Someone told him, (Your mother and your brothers are standing outside, asking to speak with you.") But he said in reply to the one who told him, "Who is my mother? Who are my brothers?" And stretching out his hand toward his disciples, he said, "Here are my mother and my brothers. For whoever does the will of my heavenly Father is my brother, and sister, and mother." (Matt 12:46-50)

As we fulfill our responsibilities in homeschooling our children with love and faithfulness, I believe Jesus sees Mary's heart in our hearts. Can we not have "a Mother Mary spirit" as we do His will? And, don't we often find that these acts of faith and obedience often involve mothering our children?

I encourage you to consider yourself in this sense and as directed by Jesus Himself, as "a little mother" of Him, and to see your little "flock" or each member of your "little flock" as a little Jesus. I believe this is our Blessed Mother's desire as well: that you draw closer to her and be grafted into her very own heart.

New Wine

And in the Gospel of Mark, Jesus tells the disciples, "Likewise, no one pours new wine into old wineskins" (Mark 2:22). What is this new wine Jesus is talking about? Is He not giving a new and different grace? And if so, what could that grace be?

Once, we were children and young adults ourselves. We loved our parents and those around us. As we matured, however, and had children of our own, our capacity to love grew and changed – it became sweeter. Many parents will tell you that the tenderness they feel in their heart for their own child(ren) is so much deeper and more sacrificial than any love they have previously known. Yes, they have deep affection for parents, siblings, extended family, and friends; but what a mother feels for each one of her children is more like an ocean, overflowing with love and grace.

Could this grace that we receive, when we become a parent, not also be considered new wine?
- A new wine in the sense that it is the ardent and sacrificial love of a parent.
- A new wine in the sense of the higher calling.

Could not the "new wine" be poured out in a continuous flow, as in the understanding heart of a parent, a pure heart that wants the best for one's children, and that abundantly shares with them the deepest resources, knowledge, and gifts? The most enduring blessing may be multi-generational fruit, as our children become vessels of new wine themselves – one day pouring into their own offspring (and even spiritual children) the love and teaching they have received. In this light such new meaning is brought to the Scripture: "but showing love down to the thousandth generation of those who love me and keep my commandments" (Exodus 20:6).

Know, dear homeschooling mother, that there is no limit to the strength, inspiration, and wisdom found in Scripture. Time spent dwelling with the Lord in pondering His Word is time well spent, indeed.

Happy pondering with Mary's heart.
Michelle

5: The Church Today

Dear Homeschooling Mom:

In looking at the Church and our culture today, we see a growing shift toward homeschooling. But it could be argued that this "movement" of mothers teaching their children actually began many years ago. What we witness today could be viewed through a different lens as a continuation of a long and beautiful history. It seems to me that our Heavenly Mother began this teaching at Lourdes, continued it at Fatima, and that still today, she shows her children the way to love – by prayer and penance. Perhaps our Blessed Mother has been "homeschooling" us, guiding us herself, preparing our hearts to be more fully able to receive her as our Mother.

The Blessed Mother's Recent Apparitions

Consider that at Lourdes in 1858, our Blessed Mother introduced herself saying, "I am the Immaculate Conception." She appeared to a young child, Saint Bernadette and invited the Church to begin anew with prayers and penances to draw close to her and her power of intercession.

Years later, in Fatima in 1917, the three children described our Blessed Mother as "a lady dressed in white," a lady of beauty and grace. She appeared with the presence and power of a queen, demonstrating her heavenly sway by obtaining the grace of the miracle of the sun. It is here that our Lady asked that Russia be consecrated to her Immaculate Heart, stating "In the end, my Immaculate Heart will triumph."

More recently, in the Medjugorje apparitions (regarding which we await the Church's final pronouncement), our Blessed Mother comes, addressing us as "Dear children." She appears as a mother to her children, and she reportedly shares her motherly heart with messages, as a mother would. Her many words of truth, guidance and wisdom always seem to me to be like short "homeschooling lessons," which I am to receive as a little child. (I submit, and urge you as well, to wait for the Church's decision regarding the authenticity of the Medjugorje apparitions, which has not been reached at this time. Mother Church knows best.)

As a homeschool mother, I encourage you to dwell richly in the approved apparitions, namely those of Guadalupe, Fatima, and Lourdes. Your heavenly mother loves you dearly and sees you growing in her image and likeness as a mother loving the "little Jesus" in your children.

Totus Tuus

We cannot help but reflect that there is a Marian movement going forward triumphantly within the Church herself. More Marian devotions grace the earth than at any other time in history, and religious orders, fraternities, and rosary groups are too numerous to count.

In addition, Saint Pope John Paul II instituted the Luminous mysteries. He took the motto *"Totus Tuus,"* Latin for totally yours, to express his personal devotion to Mary, as a beloved son. He also instituted the last Marian feast day,

Mary Mother of the Church, to be held on the Monday following Pentecost.

But of all the things Saint Pope John Paul II did, certainly one of the most important was his act of consecration, in which he consecrated the world to Her Immaculate Heart. He fulfilled this expressed desire and request of Our Blessed Mother at Fatima. He invoked her not as a queen, or as intercessor, but as a mother. In his prayer of consecration, he prays:

> O Mother of men and people, you know all their sufferings and their hopes, you feel in a motherly way all the struggles between good and evil, between the light and the darkness which shakes the world. Accept our cry addressed in the Holy Spirit directly to your heart and embrace with the love of the Mother and the Handmaid of the Lord the peoples who await this embrace the most, and likewise the peoples whose consecration you too are particularly awaiting. Take under your motherly protection the whole human family which we can consecrate to you, O mother, with affectionate rapture. May the time of peace and freedom, the time of truth, justice and hope, approach for everyone.

As you homeschool, dear mother, I encourage you to ponder this Marian movement, while considering your place in it – that, in fact, you are part of the triumph of Mary's heart in some particular manner. I believe your Blessed Mother would have it no other way.

The Gift of Homeschooling to the Church

At the present moment, there is a tremendous outpouring of the gift of homeschooling. With this gift of "mothers choosing the homeschool option" for their children, many are being drawn closer to our Blessed Mother, as they look to her as a source of inspiration, and as they choose and implement curriculum materials for formation and instruction.

As we look around and see a multiplication in new homeschooling moms, we can also look back to see the results of the labors of those homeschooling mothers, who have gone before us. These young people now are blessing the Church in abundant ways, cultivating the Church, engaging in their communities, excelling in academic pursuits, pursuing vocations, and passing on the tradition of homeschooling to their own families.

What Can We Glean from Church History?

This gift of homeschooling to the Church can be compared to the gift of Saint Francis in the 1200s when the Church needed much reform in the way of living "gospel poverty." Many priests and prelates were indulging in the luxuries of life while ignoring the Gospel. They were not following the teachings of Jesus and His example of seeking and imparting spiritual riches, but were seeking material wealth. They forgot that Jesus came in poverty and remained in poverty preaching the Good News. The Church needed to be reminded of the beauty and gift of poverty at that time, and trust in the providence of God. And God raised up Saint Francis as this beacon of light to show a better way.

As already stated, this grace of homeschooling does not mean that every parent should homeschool their child(ren). That would be like saying that every priest in the thirteenth century should have become a Franciscan. That type or radical thinking was not wise then, nor is it now. Perhaps we can serve in various ways as beacons of light in the schooling of our children at home.

We need only look to the lives of hundreds of canonized saints who were formed and educated through the traditional school systems of their time. And some saints have been canonized largely due to their love of children, manifesting itself through the founding of schools and academic institutions. Saint John Bosco, Saint Elizabeth Ann Seton, Mother Cabrini and Father Morreau come to mind.

But perhaps we can serve in various ways as beacons of light in the schooling of our children at home. What all this does mean is that the grace of homeschooling that is now being given to the Church is to tweak the Church and allow the Church to "more deeply hit the nail on the head."

This move of God can be compared to a parish pastor who, seeing that his parish needs to grow in penance or prayer, arranges for a Franciscan to come lead a retreat. He does not arrange this so that every parishioner can become a Franciscan... that would be silly. But he desires that his parish grow more deeply in prayer and penance. The priest hopes that the grace a Franciscan receives from living out his vows/promises and his charism of penance will overflow to the congregation, as the Franciscan preaches and teaches and lives among them for a few days.

Perhaps as a Church, and as faithful Catholics and Christians, we need to see this as a season to grow deeper in our faith, to have a firm foundation to support the many graces God is pouring out on us at this time in history. I encourage you, as a homeschool mother, to reflect upon these mercies, to ponder why they are being bestowed upon the Church at this time.

In the same way, by fulfilling your call to homeschool, your efforts can be a beautiful grace in this season, an aid to help the Church refocus on priorities, balance, children, and holiness. In such a way, you can be a light and resource for the entire Church, a gift from heaven above.

God Bless,
Michelle

6: Homeschooling: A Mother's Call Forward

Dear Homeschooling Mom:

I believe God is calling you higher and into a closer relationship with Him, and because of this, perhaps your most important job as a homeschooling mother is not in buying books.

Choosing and investing in a curriculum is probably where most of us begin our homeschooling journey. This certainly was true for me. I bought every kindergarten book available – to make sure I had every subject covered from phonics to math to outdoor nature studies! I "had it all," so to speak. In terms of curriculum materials for a five-year-old, I seemingly lacked nothing. So, imagine my surprise when I realized two years later, that this same child, at age seven did not know his birthday. (Yikes!)

Not only that, but somewhere around six months into homeschooling, after buying all the books, I felt hungry for more. Something in fact was lacking. All these exciting age-appropriate materials did not completely satisfy me, and I wanted more for my children. The knowledge being imparted needed a purpose. My carefully chosen curriculum seemed to lack direction, and I felt I was being called to journey higher.

God was calling me toward Him. He was (and still is) inviting me into relationship with Him. He wanted to give me a fuller "program," a full meal, not just the first course. He wanted to fill me, so that He could fill my children, as well. Perhaps you, too, feel God is taking you by the hand and inviting you to experience more of Him, so that this spiritual richness may be imparted to your children.

Forward March

God is a God of love, and it is fitting that He would desire to draw us closer to Himself. And if we are to move closer to Him, we must "leave" one place and "go" to another. A step forward, a step higher is an intentional, ordered step in a new direction.

I began to really ponder what I wanted for my children – to ask what was most important. Eventually, my heart settled on this statement – that after glorifying God and loving my spouse, my mission was my children and my goal for them was heaven.

Amidst a world of distractions, HOMESCHOOLING IS A WORLD THAT FOCUSES UPON THE CHILD and what is best for them. This is not to say that we make our children and their homeschooling little gods! It says, rather, that it is in the child's best interest that he or she be given a life built upon faith IN GOD, and all that is godly and good.

When I focus on my child(ren), and God's plan for them, I can more easily prioritize. I build from a center, which is giving my children a gift of faith.

For me, growing in the Lord and having a deeper focus in homeschooling seem to be a two-step process. First, I must answer the question WHY, and then I must identify and prioritize the curriculum in relation to my answer.

The Question of WHY

It all begins with answering this question of WHY. This WHY can be compared to an imagined scenario with a plank of wood, set across two very tall buildings. If I were to ask you to walk across the plank high above, you would most likely refuse. If I put your child on the other side of that beam, you would dash across it to bring your child to safety. We have answered the question of why: to bring our child(ren) to safety.

Homeschooling begins and continues with answering the question WHY. There is a reason we homeschool, why we willingly sacrifice our very lives day in and day out. We believe it is best for the child, and we are willing to order our lives around what is best for the one(s) entrusted to our care.

A story from the life of Mother Teresa illustrates this level of commitment. She once saw a nun with a gloomy face working with the poor and immediately "dismissed" her. This action surprised me when I first heard it recounted. I hadn't expected that Mother Teresa would be that forceful and abrupt with one of her own sisters. But, in reflection I realized that Mother Teresa held the poor in such esteem and love that she could not allow a glum personality to negatively affect their wellbeing. She wanted these already struggling individuals, now in her care, to experience only light and happiness. The "poor" were Mother Teresa's children.

Mother Teresa also recognized that her "children" included the religious sisters, with whom she served, and they, too, needed to learn from her example the importance of radiating Christ to the poor. She wanted to model this love for them and thus required consistent kindness in their dealings with the sick and dying. In this situation, Mother Teresa was a mother in the truest sense of the word, and she knew what was most important. She was not afraid to discipline – gently, quickly, and precisely – when necessary, to give her "children" the best. She wanted to give the poor a radiant reflection of Christ, and her sisters a courageous example to imitate.

We can learn much from this one example. As homeschooling mothers, we try to focus our own hearts and minds on what is most essential for our children's learning, growth, and development – and to help our children do the same.

Identifying Curriculum

The world would have us believe that curriculum is solely about books and lesson plans. And while yes, that is probably the dictionary definition, a homeschool curriculum can be designed to encompass so much more – intellectual, academic and spiritual endeavors – a whole program for the whole child. The focus should be on mental and spiritual formation, both head and heart.

Perhaps a better way to think of curriculum would be not in terms of the books you buy or the lesson plans your children complete, but more broadly to include ideas, habits, and traditions that we seek to impart. Furthermore, people, places, field trips, authors, creative projects, and even one-on-one conversations will be part of your "curriculum."

Curriculum for me, is what I want my children to study closely… to practically dwell upon. Perhaps the goal of learning is to have the essence of what is being studied engraved upon their hearts – to have it become part of them. Curriculum then is a compendium of what the children are taking in, contemplating, being exposed to, and gazing upon.

"Curriculum" is that which my child(ren) will deem worthy to use (years from now) in parenting their own child(ren). It consists of books, ideas, people, memories, and traditions that my children have come to love and, hopefully, will want to pass along to my grandchildren. Above all, curriculum is what REMAINS, what is passed along, what is treasured, and what endures.

What is in Your Basket – Selecting Your Curriculum

I am easily distracted, (squirrel!), and the one thing that I lack is time. And to make the best use of the moments, days, and years I have with my children, I need to be intentional about creating order and setting priorities. I need a fine-tuned sense of direction. Otherwise, I will just be filling my "basket" with variations of things like science projects, which might not ever get completed.

Yes, I see this gift of prioritizing a bit like filling a basket. The pretty woven container has limited space, so I must be careful about choosing what to put in there. I also see that many objects are "good," but some are better or more appropriate. In my own homeschooling journey, I began to really ponder what "food" I wanted to feed my children. Especially with so much to choose from, a mother must be selective.

This does not mean that I never put, say, silly things in the basket. But I do so as the exception, not the rule.

To help simplify areas of emphases in my mind, I jotted down lifelong learning categories, which I would like to share with you. These are the things that are closest to my heart and that I want my children to receive and embrace. This is the curriculum, broken down into the values I most cherish and want to pass on to my children.

1) Love of Prayer
2) Love of Family
3) Love of Community
4) Love of Classical Education
5) Love of a Living Education
6) Love of Creating a Living Home
7) Love of the Church

"Books" and a formal curriculum would fall under number 4 in the basket. The curriculum I personally choose to use offers much more than what we traditionally think of as academic, and these activities which involve our children often can count as "homeschooling time." A Catholic Classical Education is in my opinion the best approach, as these materials successfully teach subject matter, while incorporating a life mission of service and joy.

I encourage you to ponder the materials you want in your basket, your curriculum of choice to help your children grow into living saints filled with joy and wonder.

Happy focusing,
God Bless,
Michelle .

7: Love of Prayer

Dear Homeschooling Mom:

I invite you to drink deeply from the wellspring of prayer… it is not like you are going to need it or anything! (Wink, wink!)

Create in Me a Clean Heart

Homeschooling is very hard work, and because of the nature and duration of its challenges, the homeschool mother must become even more dependent on the Lord. She may find herself more often on her knees in prayer seeking His grace, strength, and guidance. When the Lord gives you a big God-sized vision to bring up holy and righteous children, He also gifts you with an extraordinary need for His wisdom and grace.

This is part of my experience. As a young mother, I frequently felt frustrated, even overwhelmed, as I juggled the demands of homeschooling with the ever present (and equally important) needs of my younger children. Yet, the Lord had given me such a beautiful picture of the end result – my hopes and dreams for my children – that I could only keep moving forward.

Even so, I remember feeling helpless and unqualified. At times, this vulnerability would be quite evident, for instance, as I begged my husband not to leave for work until we'd said family prayers together. I deeply sensed the grace that came from even briefly gathering our little flock to invite God into our day. I remember desperately needing God in those early years, and I still need Him, even more.

"My grace is sufficient for you, for power is made perfect in weakness" (2 Cor 12:9).

Through prayer in the quiet moments, we see what is most important. In this holy stillness, we grow in patience, peace, and perseverance – all motherly character traits. God enfolds our heart, and as He does, we become softer and more docile. I find that as God takes me by the hand, leading me on my journey, I thirst for more of this Holy Spirit guidance.

Morning Personal Prayer and Inspirational Reading

In my desire and search for God, I attended a retreat in which the leader shared with us about one of her personal Lenten journeys – one that she had found particularly life-changing. She described how she had felt led to devote the first hour of each day to just one thing – thanking the Lord. She went on to recount the fruit from this discipline, saying that by the end of Lent, she was "an entirely different person." With children ages six, five, and two at the time, she admitted that it had been challenging. Yet, she had persevered! I was inspired. Yet, I couldn't help thinking, "really Lord, a whole hour?"

After my time of renewal and hearing this message, I felt led to honor the Lord by giving Him an hour each morning at the start of my day. With a houseful of young children (by nature early risers), this meant I had to get up at the crack of dawn, long before what I considered normal or even possible. Yet, God provided the grace, and He has remained faithful ever since. My time with the Lord is so precious to Him and to me.

During these moments of quiet, I also engage in inspirational reading, and I commit to journaling. Looking back over the years, it is beautiful to see my shelf lined with books that have accompanied me along my journey. This time was not without interruptions, and often I could read only a page or two, or sometimes even just a paragraph. But gradually, I waded through the pages, finding inspiration and growing in Biblical knowledge and wisdom.

Homeschooling is a beautiful movement, and it is made even more powerful in each family when the mother prays. Through her tenaciousness and accompanying joy, the whole family is led closer to Jesus. The mother can only survive through regular times of prayer.

Hearing God's Voice

When I think of prayer, the gift probably most dearest to my heart, and that which I want most to pass on to my children, is that of discerning the voice of the Lord. What does His voice sound like? How do we listen to and hear the voice of God? The world says that God's voice is harsh, loud, and critical, but I have found that it is so gentle, humble, and full of understanding. It is always full of hope and love. It is a voice that carries these characteristics, giving direction not only through the words themselves, but in how they are spoken, often humbly and gently. Even with words that convict or correct, the conviction comes with a message of hope and encouragement.

I want my children to come to know, hear, and desire to always follow God's voice. It is one of the most important tasks I have as a mother, guiding them toward this understanding and cultivating this desire in their hearts.

Once we have learned to recognize the gentle whisper of God (see 1 Kings 19:12), we can lead others to hear His voice. We can gently inspire them to sit before Him in an attitude of graciousness with an open heart, ready to respond. God is always speaking to us, always giving us words of love and encouragement, indeed always singing over us: "My sheep hear my voice; I know them, and they follow me" (John 10:27).

This intimacy with the Lord can be further developed in many ways and at various times and places: on a nature walk, in a solemn, quiet church, during a family dinner, or reading Scripture aloud. What is important is to create those times and spaces, and to seek Him with an attitude that is receptive and ready to catch a glimpse of God.

These moments, especially with younger children, can be eagerly anticipated. There is great joy in knowing that God is speaking to their precious hearts. This art of listening for and hearing the voice of God can be grasped gradually, maybe fifteen seconds at a time. But when these little ones become teenagers and the world is competing for their attention, this practice of prayer will serve and protect them well. Their hearts and minds will already be opened and attuned to God.

Family Rosary

Looking back, I can see the hand of the Lord in my seasons of greatest vulnerability. It was at one of those times of weakness, when I turned to the Lord in daily morning prayer, and the Lord began moving in our family in a powerful way. We were inspired to begin our morning family prayer and later the family rosary. I see countless ways the Lord, through the intercession of the Blessed Mother, rained down graces upon our family – graces of devotions, favorite family saints, and the creation of family traditions.

Our family rosary was difficult to implement, but we are all so thankful we persevered. Saying the rosary is easy; saying the rosary as a family is more challenging.

As we stumbled and fell, we rose to our feet again, metaphorically speaking, God blessed our efforts in every way. Looking back, and contemplating our path, I would suggest that a family with young children set a goal of saying the rosary for fifteen minutes, and not worry about where it ends. Praying the entire rosary would be ideal, but a half hour in prayer with little ones may not be realistic (unsolicited advice here!). Have no doubt, families do grow in maturity, and soon the family is able to say the entire rosary beautifully. Know that sometimes, however, it is a journey to get to this point, and the interruptions are a wonderful part of the journey.

Daily Mass

Shortly after this time, my children and I also were drawn to daily Mass. With young active homeschool kids, this seemed an impossible undertaking. And yet, how the Lord rewarded my faithfulness and desire! He "raised up" an older lady, who sat next to my oldest son, to become like a second grandmother to him. The Lord also gave my daughter a "grandfather" in whom she absolutely delighted, seeing him weekly at Wednesday Mass.

I marveled as I watched the Lord create situations, through which my children thrived in the congregation. Eventually, they enjoyed altar serving, music ministry, and Eucharistic Ministry. We also made so many friends.

I came to believe that the gift of presenting our children to the Lord each day at Mass is the greatest gift I could give them. We tried to begin attending the sacrifice of the Holy Mass on most school days, and I asked the Lord to teach, guide, and enfold their hearts. He is the divine teacher. We all received abundant graces from this ritual. I never regretted going to Mass with my children, although admittedly keeping my focus, and gently nudging them to do the same was always "part and parcel" of this spiritual start to our day.

In my journey, I came across a story which really strengthened my resolve to attend daily Mass with my children. It spoke to their hearts as well, and I will share it with you. Well-known Catholic author and speaker, Matthew Kelly, once recounted the story of a priest who traveled to China on holiday.

This father did not travel in clerical garb, so upon his arrival at a particular village, no one knew he was, in fact, a Catholic priest. One night he awoke to the sound of murmuring and whispering. People were saying, "the wall… we are going to the wall." As they headed out to a forested area, he followed quietly behind. And, when men began climbing trees in a clearing, the priest was completely bewildered. The mystery continued, as silence and stillness came over the gathering. Then, one in the group walked up to "the wall" in the middle of the clearing and removed a single stone: it revealed the Eucharist in a hidden monstrance. All knelt down in prayer before Jesus.

The next morning, the priest asked the villagers about what had happened the night before. They shared with him that they were keeping the faith alive, but had not had Mass celebrated in ten years. The priest revealed his vocation to them, and later that night they made the same trek to the wall, though this time with great anticipation. With overwhelming joy, these villagers participated in the Sacrifice of the Holy Mass for the first time in ten years. And, for the father, it was one of the high points of his priesthood.

I also find a "living education" in the sacrifice of the Mass, especially when I slow down and ponder the beauty and truth within each holy Communion. Every day, the liturgical calendar is filled with saints' feasts, quotes from giants in the faith, and wisdom from great theologians. If I focus on only one word of a homily (which has happened on more occasions than I can count), that "word" becomes pivotal to my day.

Mass Candy

Yes, you guessed it – I did reward (bribe?) my children with candy as a sweet incentive to pay attention during Mass, and I've never regretted it. I wanted them to be listening and expecting that good things were coming – both in spiritual rewards and yes, candy in the car!

After Mass, we made a game of it, with small pieces of chocolate (like chocolate chips) given out for answers to any or all of the following questions:

1: What was the meaning in the first reading?
2: What was the Psalm response?
3: What was the Gospel about?
4: What did the priest say in the homily?
5: Was this a saint's feast day?
6: How did Jesus touch their own heart during Mass? (This is the best question).

I can live with six or seven chocolate bits in exchange for increased focus, and ultimately more spiritual hunger. My kids came to enjoy the activity and learned to be prepared for the drive home.

I encourage you to consider the beauty of the sacrifice of Mass a bit more deeply. It is the most sacred and full education you can receive and give to your child(ren). Mass contains order, liturgy, Scripture readings, Bible stories, reasoning, and so much more. But most importantly, it is God's gift to you dear homeschool mother… for your strength for the journey.

Mother's Sabbath

The Lord led me to know that He desired for me to take a Mother's Sabbath during the week. When the children were little, I could only take one- or two-hour breaks once or twice a week, rather than an entire day. These were comprised of attending a weekly evening prayer group, and exercising on Sunday, when I would squeeze in a run – yes, the kind with jogging shoes on a path or track! During those two "outings," the Lord blessed my "away time" with Him, and I left those events feeling inspired and refreshed. It was also wonderful for my children to be away from me for a bit. We all needed that break.

I also believe I was able to embrace the calling to have more children with the balance of a Sabbath. My heart was open because I was able to rest a bit, and this gave me the courage to obey this leading with joy. These were holy and sacred times for me, and I encourage you to consider how you might experience times of refreshment with God.

Family Devotions

As I began reading and seeking the Lord in prayer, I was inspired to create a family culture where the Catholic faith thrived. The recognition of saints filled our home with the feast day of a family saint; the joyful expectation of Advent, the embracing of Lenten practices, and of course Christmas and Easter celebrations. Yes, our family loves to celebrate.

During my husband's and my early parenting days, I now realize the Lord was laying the foundation from which family traditions would take root and spring up. I would try to sow the seeds of one or two activities a year, following the inspiration of this or that. And before I knew it, those sweet "little activities" had grown into family traditions which the whole family looked forward to. Looking back, it is heartening to see how individual seeds of our own family culture blossomed into beautiful plants – special traditions that bring forth fruit annually.

Dear mother, I hope that the reflections I have shared are helpful in some way, wherever you are in your faith walk. This has been an important part of my spiritual growth, over sixteen years of homeschooling through both peaks and valleys. I can only pray that these meditations are a source of inspiration and encouragement to you. God meets us where we are and always gives us the next step. Have no fear, "for the Lord your God goes with you; he will never leave you or forsake you" (Deuteronomy 31:6).

God Bless,
Michelle

8: Love of Family (I): Growing in Holiness with One's Spouse

Dear Homeschool Mom:

Your marriage is one of God's greatest gifts to you. It is a sacrament, which gives grace to you, your husband, and your children. It is also an outward sign to all around you. Sacramental graces flow out from your marriage, upon you, your children, and your community. These graces flow daily. You receive the gift to love one another "as one body in Christ," and the grace to lay down your life for each other, as the two of you become one. In marriage, parents also receive the grace to lay down their lives for their children.

My Own Journey to Nuptials

I met my husband at Saint Mary's College in Notre Dame, Indiana. We had a beautiful dating season on the picturesque Notre Dame and Saint Mary's campuses. This season was followed by a time of patient waiting and a two-year, long-distance relationship. Eventually, we could not stand the physical and geographical separation any longer, and we decided it was time to marry!

We have been blessed with twenty-five years of marriage and six children (two of whom abide in heaven after sadly losing them through miscarriage). Together, we are an active family with many deep interests and passions.

My Gift to My Husband

Love is desiring the best for another and striving to accomplish it. To truly fulfill my vocation in marriage, I want the best for my husband. My heart's desire for him is the highest degree of glory in heaven – to be an image that God the Father looks at and delights in. I want the Father to be so pleased with my husband and to see His image and likeness in my spouse. This is my greatest hope for Chris, and I daily strive to take steps to actively assist him, as he walks in his faith journey. (Hopefully this does not play out by my being his cross to bear, although at times I am sure that is the case!). In short, I must be a blessing, a prayer partner, and a straight arrow pointing him toward heaven – always with the message that he is loved and cherished.

I also want the best for him in this life. He has such talent in so many areas, and I enjoy seeing him grow in all his giftings. I want my husband to be successful in whatever directions and pursuits he chooses. The things that are important to him are important to me.

Finally, with all the stress and distractions in today's world, I want my husband to have a safe haven, a home, and a place where he can peacefully dwell – secure in knowing he is truly loved and cherished by his family. I want him to be able to look at me and understand that goodness and kindness surround him, and that I have his best interests at heart. I want our home and our marriage to be a little piece of heaven on earth for him to dwell in.

Delighting in My Husband

I admire so much about Chris – as a husband and a father and as a man of God. Any time I devote to dwelling upon his characteristics and virtues is time well spent. As I contemplate these fingerprints of God in my spouse, I discover more and more about him. I easily make these beautiful observations as he interacts daily with our kids, rises to the occasion in various work situations, and so much more. It is also so much fun to celebrate him with birthdays, anniversaries, and date nights because there is much to celebrate! A lifetime is too short to fully discover each other.

Listening to His Heart

I always had thought that women had "larger," more understanding hearts than men. But this idea was quickly put to rest some years ago when my husband and I attended a Marriage Encounter retreat (which I highly recommend). Part of the weekend consists in writing letters to one's spouse. Through this letter writing process, I discovered a depth of my husband's heart beyond what I'd known existed! I discerned that I was married to a man whom I had only just begun to fully appreciate. I more completely comprehended the truth in the Scripture, "God made man in his own image" (Genesis 1:27). I also was impressed by how many other women on this retreat expressed the same surprise and appreciation, as they read their own special notes from their husbands.

Spending Time with Your Spouse

I encourage you to take time simply to be with your spouse. These moments are like precious jewels that over time fill a box with treasured memories. They are minutes, hours, days that you spend willingly, often at great sacrifice. And this offering says "I love you" more than any ring, bracelet, or necklace ever could.

In our busy culture, a husband and wife can easily succumb to moving forward in the same direction, but on different tracks. While this can be good in specific ways on certain days, it is better for both to be on the same train, traveling together toward the identical destination. God desires that we interweave our lives around each other. "His" goals become my goals, and likewise "my" priorities or inspirations are his in some way – and he will help me accomplish them. In this way, "the two become one."

I also have pondered that as we are "one body in Christ," any decision I make will impact him in some way. It makes me pause before launching into any "heroic" endeavor.

Communication

Communication is at the heart of every marriage relationship, and good communication is key to two people growing in union. Our spouse needs to hear from our heart. Sometimes, as women, it is hard to get to the crux of a particular matter, and especially when we are already on overload with too much spinning in our brains.

And, on occasion, we may learn in what manner to best communicate by learning how NOT to communicate – been there, done that – and temper tantrums don't work, either. Neither does walking away. What, I find, does move the dialogue forward, is openly and honestly sharing what is on my heart.

The Lord led Chris and I to create a "quiet room" (actually it is the laundry room), where we can converse about an issue "off-site" away from "little people," who want a voice in the discussion. With God's help, we have found a way that works well. There, we face each other, hold hands, and express our aggravation with a situation, person, or behavior. Thus, I can truly place my hands in his, and his in mine, while simply saying, "I am frustrated with …." Though there risks associated with being open and honest, it is through this vulnerability that God often gives us great clarity. And, yes humility is required. Afterward, one of us will add a prayer, "Lord we come to you again, and we ask that you intervene in this situation."

Bumps in the Road

Every marriage is a journey, and in each journey we encounter bumps along the way. Initially, I was fearful of these jolts, but I have discovered that God allows them in His timing and for His purposes, as part of the path we walk. And, I have found "more" in these obstacles, realizing they are often there to be embraced rather than avoided.

Along one of these rougher stretches, Chris and I met with a priest who gave us some sage advice, once again. Then God blessed us with even more. In prayer, He gave us a "prescription" for how to grow in our marriage, which we have found to be solid advice that yields fruit.

It consists of five practices to make high priorities in building our marriage:

1) The first fifteen minutes when a spouse returns from work belongs to the couple as they share their day together as they reconnect as husband and wife. The couple sits down by themselves and shares their day with each other. This helps them reconnect after the hours apart, whether those were eventful, stressful, happy, discouraging, life-changing, or routine. This takes a bit of training of one's children in the beginning, but they come to respect this as Mom's and Dad's "alone time."

2) Each month, the couple needs a date night. It doesn't have to be anything fancy, just time set aside in a place away from the normal scene.

3) Once a year, the couple needs an overnight from 11:00 am to 11:00 am – a full twenty-four hours. One scenario is for the husband to select the dates and location and for the wife to arrange for the childcare.

4) Once a year, the couple needs a long weekend (Friday afternoon to Sunday morning). Once again, the husband sets the time and chooses the place, while the wife arranges the childcare. This was the suggestion of the priest, and we have had fun with Chris surprising me with the location.

5) Try to end every night holding hands and praying with and over one another.

Frank and Ruby

Another image I would like to share with you is a "real-life" portrait of what marriage can be. Frank and Ruby were married for over sixty years, and it was said that they had never had a fight. This was a real couple who were part of our parish. So, I asked Frank one day if this peaceful wedlock that they were known for was indeed the truth. He responded, yes, adding, "Well, I just loved her too much to ever fight with her." She felt the same way toward him. Their children attest to the fact that they absolutely never fought, but always met challenges and made decisions by simply discussing what was at hand. Love for each other just exuded from them both. I believe this is the marriage to which the Lord calls each of us. And while married life can be far from this ideal, somehow I believe that keeping the ideal in mind can lead to less conflict.

Vision for our children

Lastly, as this is a book for homeschooling mothers, as they teach their children, we want our marriages to be strong – to give our children a bright vision of this God-instituted foundation for the family. We want them to seek out loving partners, having observed first-hand what real love looks like. If they know what a "healthy "marriage is, then they will naturally gravitate toward healthy relationships.

Homeschool families, by the very nature of the mother sacrificing her own career to be home, are most often two-parent families. Being surrounded by other families with both a mother and a father in the house can be another benefit to homeschooled kids.

For us, it has been a tremendous blessing to be able to surround our children with families that exemplify healthy marriages. My oldest child was eleven before he even knew the meaning of the word divorce, and only years later did he actually know a family experiencing the pain of this break-up. I never tried to shield him (or my other children) from these realities, but this was just the environment the Lord willed to create for them. They were able to grow and thrive among wonderful homeschooling families. The entire community just grew up together.

Single Parent Families or Families Suffering from a Less-than-Ideal Situation

If you are a single mom or a mother struggling in your marriage, my heart goes out to you. Homeschooling is tough enough with two dedicated parents – and that much more challenging for anyone walking this path on your own. However, I believe in the power of God and the power of prayer. He provides and does so with abundance during especially difficult times. You and your family are in my heart and prayers.

I wanted to share with you some of my own story that will hopefully bring encouragement. While I have not walked in your shoes, experience has taught me about the provision of God as Father. When I was just sixteen years old, my father passed away from cancer. At times, the journey was hard, and sometimes still is, especially during milestone moments. However, what I have come to recognize is how God always provided a father figure in my life, even up to the present moment. Yes, God the Father has placed these "father" figures in my life at exactly the right times, each one bringing the perfect gift of "fatherly wisdom when I needed those graces most. And, I believe that Father God has allowed me to draw even closer to Him, precisely because I needed more of His presence due to the loss of my earthly father. Yes, this father-daughter relationship has looked different, but it has been no less valued or real. I believe the Lord can do the same for you as a single or struggling parent by surrounding you with special graces – ideal situations and individuals to meet every need.

A fatherly "figure" taught me how to drive, and I will be forever grateful to him. How I took to the road and mastered this skill in his Camaro! My brother walked me down the aisle. My father-in-law has provided much-needed direction and wisdom during times of uncertainty. And, each of my children, through our church family, has been blessed by friendships with grandfatherly figures, who showered them love – seemingly hand-picked for this role in their lives. God has always provided exactly what my children and I needed, and part of the journey has been discovering and enjoying His provision.

I encourage you to think about how even in the midst of the trials and struggles of a less-than-ideal situation, God is still providing His unique support and encouragement. It may look different than what is typical or anticipated, but if it is from the Lord, it is the most perfect gift, singularly designed for you and your children.

Homeschooling mother, I pray that you will cultivate your relationship with your husband and delight in him. Cherish him. I pray for you, to have the grace to become "one" in mind, heart, and spirit."

God Bless,
Michelle

9: Love of Family (II): The Gift of Family

Dear Homeschooling Mom:

The domestic church is the foundation upon which society is built. What a powerful thought! The work you are doing is just that important – the family is the bedrock of our society and of the larger Church. The structures, mindset, and priorities that you put in place now will bear fruit for generations to come. The values that you are living and teaching will guide your children as they enter the world. And, eventually they, too, will employ these same biblical principles and convictions, as they shape new social structures, refortify traditional mores, and point the way to a sound and hopeful path in a world that has gone astray.

The Catechism states in the section titled, The Domestic Church: "In our own time, in a world often alien and even hostile to faith, believing families are of primary importance as centers of living radiant faith. . . .Thus the home is the first school of Christian life and 'a school for human enrichment.'" (CCC: 1656-1657).

Defining Family

The Merriam-Webster dictionary defines family as "the basic unit in society, traditionally consisting of two parents rearing their children" (see: https://www.merriam-webster.com/dictionary/family). But in truth, family is so much more. I believe it has the potential to truly and beautifully go far beyond that definition. Family involves tradition and a time and place in history, as well as unity, understanding, and a sense of belonging. It provides connection and positive communication. Most importantly it creates lasting relationships.

Time with Family

One of the reasons many choose to homeschool is to create a schedule and environment that lends itself to spending time together as a family. We all want our children to develop a closeness to their siblings and to maintain those special relationships as they grow older. We also want them to know and hear our "voice" and continue to remember it years later, as they take their first steps into the world. This collective wisdom is built upon strong, life-giving relationships. Family connectedness is a gift to our children, and we will all reap the rewards of stewarding this gift with care. (Of course, I say this with the understanding that healthy relationships need to be nurtured and unhealthy ones addressed through pruning, regrowth, direction, and cutting, if needed.)

Time with family is precious indeed, and we all know it should be a high priority. However, it can be tempting sometimes to give more attention to our contacts in the athletic, artistic, or academic arenas at the expense of quality family time. But sooner or later, we come to the realization that this form of neglect does not "end well." It is our family relationships that we most want to be deep and lasting.

I desire that my children really know both their nuclear and extended family and enjoy spending time with them. This is especially important to my heart, and we try to be intentional in our activities to build these bonds. Walks, family dinners, and family prayer provide some opportunities – as do various social activities. Each of these little moments adds to the building of something beautiful. They are potentially hidden gems, that when strung together become an unbroken thread of sparkling jewels. They gain so much from these seemingly daily or special "events" – wisdom, understanding, a sense of belonging, and an abiding knowledge that they are not alone. They know we journey together. And as with so much in the homeschool life, consistency is the key – not the size or novelty or once-in-a-lifetime nature of what we do, but just being together often!

Family History

Children need both roots and wings. Roots can ground us and keep us where we need to be – in the right soil for healthy growth. It seems so important to have time during the year to celebrate the gift of family history. Whether it is a family tree, or family stories, family members' peculiarities or similarities – all these have the potential to be noticed, nurtured, and when appropriate built upon in the lives of our children.

We give our offspring so many gifts when we share with them the accomplishments of their family members and their ancestors. Some say that generational sin can be passed down, but how much MORE can generational blessings be passed along. Career paths, talents, and certain "inclinations" can all be acknowledged and expanded in our children. Little conversations of "Wow, your grandmother was a nurse, you might be following in her footsteps," or "you and your uncle have the same birthday" can all have meaning. With God there are no coincidences, and these little bequests can bring identity and point a child in the right direction. They also serve as confirmations and take on new or different meanings, as children age.

Family Traditions and Celebrations

Developing family traditions is also so important. These little seasonal, religious, or even daily customs build a sense of uniqueness about one's own family, as well as the stability that goes with certain patterns. Traditions become friends to our soul – little lights to guide us through a cloudy world. And there is so much to be celebrated. In this world where everything seems to travel at the speed of light and all can seem fuzzy, celebrations are so foundational. Accomplishments cry out to be celebrated in some way, as do birthdays, anniversaries, baptismal days, and liturgical feast days. We seem to live a higher calling when we embrace the joy of celebration. We can also remember that all the angels and saints are in a perpetual life of celebration.

Young families are especially called to establish traditions. In so doing, we lay a rich foundation that becomes familiar and smooth over time. These "practices" are like little stepping-stones, discovered and placed along the path each year. A family Advent tree, a Lenten tradition, and so much more make for special, even sacred activities as we journey through a particular season. We know the way, because we have been here before. Meaningful customs and events strategically placed, seasonally or annually, yield such fruit, and they allow for continued creativity as families grow and our destinies unfold.

More seasoned families (I will not say older) have the task of persevering in continuing the traditions they have started. As we age, it can be tempting to skip or abbreviate this or that. But due diligence to what has been established bears such fruit. And our kids find such joy in remembering and even beginning to implement these traditions themselves.

I encourage you, dear homeschool mom, to ponder the gift of family, of your immediate and extended family and how this extraordinary God-given blessing can best be nurtured and passed on to your child(ren). As each family is different, each one will find their own unique path, as it unfolds, and together they will become the family they were meant to be.

God Bless,
Michelle

10: Love of Community

Dear Homeschooling Mom:

This chapter is one of my favorites, and writing it brought me great joy. The little Franciscan in me loves fellowship. There is just a certain part of all of us that comes alive in community. I pray that you will be blessed by the experiences and insights I share here.

When homeschool moms and families join together for the purpose of nurturing and forming their children, something wonderful happens. I believe God builds a little city of heaven right here on earth through these varied homeschooling communities.

Our Family's Journey

In our family's journey, we have been part of several different homeschool groups, the type and size depending on my children's needs and preferences at the time. When they were younger, for instance, we latched onto a faithful "park day." This simple outdoor commitment continued for over ten years.

Every Tuesday afternoon, six families (give or take a few) would gather simply for the purpose of letting the children play. This became a blessed, almost sacred, time for the kids as they ran and jumped and made noise all over the familiar, natural, open spaces. It became like a neighborhood. Truly, our children grew up together – indeed our entire families "grew up" together. The moms from those weekly park days are still some of my closest friends. We laughed and cried and inspired one another.

When I needed more of a schedule for my active older children, the Lord placed us in a hybrid community, where I received so much grace through both structure and a classical curriculum, as well as fellowship with strong, virtuous families. With a hybrid also comes the need for a bit of discipline, so the kids don't just run wild in their new environment! My children grew from some of the new expectations and focus on excellence.

Some options are only for a season, and the beautiful thing about homeschooling is the flexibility – the freedom to try new models and take new paths. When that particular "hybrid" disbanded due to various challenges, a new group was formed. This time, ten moms came together and miraculously agreed on curriculum, structure, and direction. This community thrived, and there was such joy and wonder in the children. The kids truly enjoyed bringing art, drama, writing, science, and other subjects to life … we even were visited by a horse one day.

One of the most beautiful and consistent gifts in this cooperative effort came through a faithful and "homeschool supportive" priest, who offered an engaging Mass each week for the children. Our homeschooled students truly saw Christ alive in this beloved and holy priest, and they grew in their own knowledge of and enthusiasm for their faith.

We have also walked joyfully with one more local Christian community. The budding writer in my middle schooler needed to burst forth, and we found this inspiration, as well as great community, in a Christian hybrid where that was an atmosphere of such love and acceptance among them, a sense of Christ reigning in hearts.

God has woven a unique fabric of friendships through these individual communities and contacts over this seventeen-year journey. We feel so blessed to have touched the lives of others and to have been touched in more ways than we can count. We will always value these special relationships – with all those who have walked with us during various homeschool school years and seasons. How could we not?

Blessings of Community

In all these homeschool communities, I have observed that the mothers exhibit an inexhaustible fountain of joy and inspiration, which arises from hearts of love. Personally, I am so grateful for each one the Lord has placed in my life. They accept me for who I am and for who I am not. God gives homeschooling moms such wisdom, calmness, sensitivity, order, humor, and a love of the Church, among so many other gifts. (I don't mean that those gifts are exclusive to homeschool moms, but some days it does seem that we need and receive an extra measure of these graces.)

Some of my biggest cheerleaders have been these fellow homeschooling moms. In fact, the person who is editing this book (hello Patt!), is a veteran homeschool mother. She has been one of my biggest (and calmest) encouragers. I can only pray that you, dear reader, and all who have walked this path with me will be similarly blessed. And I pray that your fruit and mine – our homeschooled children – will in turn bear much fruit in their own lives and families, in their churches and faith communities, and wherever they serve. Bless them Lord, bless them abundantly.

Gift of a Safe Environment

Children are especially blessed in like-minded communities and families. With all the chaos in the world, I am thankful that the Lord gave my children a "safe haven" in which to thrive. Because I knew the other mothers' "hearts" in our homeschool communities – that their hearts were for their children, I felt so at ease with playdates, friendships, and all the rest. I hope they felt likewise. The kids felt known and understood; they felt embraced, encouraged and nurtured by all these wonderful mothers.

Gift of a Creative Playground

Each homeschool community could well be described as a creative playground. Imagine that! I have found no lack of inspiration and initiative among these fellow parents and educators. We want our children to have the best, we will go to great lengths to see that their needs are met, and we have no problem sacrificing to make their dreams a reality. I have been amazed, for instance, at the level of work that can go into a drama production to make it "just a step down" from "Broadway," or the hoops mothers are willing to jump through to procure a reasonably priced field trip to a science museum. Mothers inspire other moms, and the creativity and resourcefulness are just contagious. For instance, I am reminded of the effort and imagination that went into an All Saints' Day party with costumes, games, skits, and more. We called it, "Let's Celebrate the Saints," and miraculously the saints did indeed join us.

Strength in Numbers

Finally, when we journey together, we all journey farther. I've always wanted my children to have the understanding that our Church is strong and united and a force to be reckoned with. It's not that I was trying to instill a sense of the control, but instead a sense of truth – to know that our Almighty God walks with the Church. I want them to feel strong, united, and part of something bigger than they could ever imagine.

Saint John Chrysostom once described the beauty of community. He wrote, "You cannot pray at home as at church, where there is a great multitude, where exclamations are cried out to God as from one great heart, and where there is something more: the union of minds, the accord of souls, the bond of charity."

I encourage you, dear Homeschooling Mother, to make every effort to become active in a homeschooling community. It may involve some exploring and even experimenting, but the potential blessings which await you are too numerous to count. Yes, it will require sacrifice on your part, but you will discover that as a true vessel of the Lord, living waters will flow from you, as you engage in a homeschool community. And, I believe you and your children will drink abundantly from "fountains" of this life-giving water.

God bless,
Michelle

11: Love of a Classical Education

Dear Homeschooling Mom:

I invite you to delve into excellence and tradition. Classical Education is built upon centuries of successful academic endeavors aimed at aiding a student in his/her journey toward excellence. This journey often includes striving for and achieving goals that seem unobtainable. But there is a key to this student success, and it's found in the manner in which goals are pursued – in an orderly progression, with consistency and focus, thought, and direction.

(I must first admit that I am no expert in regard to this traditional mode of educating students with an emphasis on liberal arts. I share my thoughts about Classical Education from the perspective of what has worked for our family, not from a position of expertise – I leave that to the professionals.)

However, I will offer here, at the start, one "professional definition" that I like from the Circe Institute:

CLASSICAL EDUCATION is the cultivation of wisdom and virtue by nourishing the soul on truth, goodness, and beauty by means of the seven liberal arts and the four sciences. so that in Christ the student is better able to know, glorify, and enjoy God. (https://www.circeinstitute.org/; from the Circe Institute with an addition from Andrew Kern)

What is Classical Curriculum?

I believe Classical curriculum is best described by saying, "Love is the education… a Classical Education is the best academic tool." Classical Education trains the mind to engage with the heart, so that a noble course of action may be identified and pursued. It is a form of academic endeavor that trains the student's focus and attention upwards toward the good, the true, and the beautiful. It aims to gather wisdom so that what is gleaned may be studied and learned, and the "perfect" wisdom may then be applied in any given situation. This process of learning and applying wisdom and knowledge allows the soul to act in a beautiful and proportionate, yet powerful way in the present moment.

Perhaps the best example is from Christ Himself. Consider the first words of Jesus as He is found in the temple. Our Lord proclaims with one powerful sentence the truth about the first person of the Holy Trinity . . .God is Father: "Did you not know that I must be in my FATHER'S house?" (emphasis mine) (Luke 2:48).

His response is ordered and powerful, and it lives in the present moment. With one sentence, Jesus's first recorded sentence brings an entire revelation about God as Father and Jesus as the Son of His Father in MY Father's house. In a sense, Jesus's entire mission is proclaimed in this sentence – a revelation of the relationship between Father and Son.

A Classical Education Begins with Wonder

Laura Berquist, founder of Mother of Divine Grace Academy, says that Classical Education begins with awe (https://modg.org/articles/2017-10-23/classical-education---

beginning-in-wonder-ending-in-wisdom). It is the moment the child pauses and allows his or her attention to gaze upon an element of the sacred, the precious, the highest, the most detailed, or a noble character, a beautiful flower, a breathtaking view, and a harmonious sound. Wonder is the moment where there is an encounter with something that is "beyond." For example, a sense of wonder fills a mountain climber upon arriving at the highest peak, or when a scientist questions why the cell is circular. It is the point at which discovery is about to be made, deeper understanding gained, and a truth understood.

With wonder, the child is ready to learn. The child readily encounters this wonder stumbling upon, or dwelling upon, the good, the true and the beautiful. The mind, connected with the soul, inquires, and God is ready to respond with the next step, the next thought, the next instruction, and the next understanding.

One knows that a child has arrived at a moment of wonder, not when he has found the right answer, but when she has discovered the right question. "I wonder why birds sing"; "I wonder how butterflies change through metamorphosis"; "I wonder why Pope Pius X lowered the age of first communicants?" With wonder, the child springs forward. Questions of this type lead the child forward towards discovery.

The Good

In our crazy world, where so much is "thrown away" in the desire to obtain more, "the good" arises, in contrast, as a "found treasure" to be cherished. One might associate this "good" with the "treasure buried in a field" and " a pearl of great price" that Jesus speaks about in Matthew 13:44-46. He likens these unearthed gems to the kingdom of heaven. In each of these parables, we are told that the one who makes the discovery of great value, sells all he has to take possession of his new-found treasure. In a nutshell, the good is priceless, and once it has been revealed, other "lesser" goods are discarded in favor of this more perfect good.

In academics, the "Good" can be a particular way of solving math problems, such as the logical reasoning in geometry steps. Or, it may be the manner of writing an essay, perhaps persuasively to make a point. These academic pursuits can be "good." The soul is at rest. One knows the good when one has discovered something upon which to build – or continue building once the foundation has been laid.

The True

Clarity and simplicity accompany what is true. The true has a ring all its own. One knows truth has been encountered, not by its complexity, but by its simplicity and ease of understanding. Saint Patrick most readily spoke of the truth of the Trinity in simplicity using a metaphor of the shamrock. A design of three smaller leaves unified in the one larger shamrock points to the truth of the Trinity – three divine Persons in one God. In the True, the soul can see into the spiritual realm with the eyes of faith. And, what is then discerned is unquestionably real. "It" exists, or more profoundly "God" exists, and the truths of God are "real."

The Beautiful

The beautiful arises from creation, the created world, or a piece of art which one has created reflecting the created world. In nature, there is so much beauty, so much order, so much wisdom. A butterfly, a delicate flower, and a sunset all reflect part of the creative Heart of God. A pond has so many vibrant orchestrated parts – the insects, animals, flowers, and plants all living in harmony. Likewise, a painting of a sunset also reflects this beauty. The beautiful is part of

God's creation, and therefore an expression, in some way, of God Himself, of His very nature....of His very Heart.

Purpose of Classical Education

If the goal of education is to form a child's mind and heart to love in profound ways, then it follows that what fills a child's heart, mind and soul must be what is deepest, highest, most ordered, and most noble. Classical Education is directed upwards; it has a higher goal and teaches one "how" to think, act, and speak. This is in contrast to some modern academic approaches that aim to teach a child "what to think."

Classical Education includes, but is not limited to, studying or at least being exposed to writings of the saints and the Church, as well as classical and historical works of fiction. These literary works are written from the viewpoint of a single author and immerse the reader into that particular time period. Classical Education includes: reading literature to enjoy, imitate, and study; building proficiency in math, one step at a time through simplicity and order; learning the derivation of words through the study of Latin; finding God's design in natural science; discovering rhythm in poetry and harmony in music – and so much more

Memorization

Memorization serves a purpose by disciplining the mind to acquire desired knowledge in a purposeful and ordered way. Memorization of the Ten Commandments is a wonderful example. God ordained that they be written in order, with the highest, most important commandment as the First Commandment, "You shall have no other gods before me" (Deuteronomy 5:6). From this experience of memorization, the child not only learns about God's "laws," but also how to articulate and speak in a determined manner. And through practice in speaking and writing, our students learn how to make an effective presentation, to put forth a thesis followed by other supporting statements. Through memorization, he or she also learns what can be discarded. Again, there is purpose and order, mission and sequence.

Building on Developmental Stages

Because Classical Education is ordered, it can move forward in sync with the developmental stages of the child. Children are naturally growing and maturing, and not to see the beauty in each stage could lead to missing certain gifts that need to be nurtured. Each season of growth is meant to be treasured and delighted in. Babies are naturally explorative, toddlers travel, and preschoolers ask WHY. In an academic scenario, children have mental abilities that are always unfolding.

First graders naturally enjoy memorization and song. They love to repeat choruses and rhymes. They have no problem memorizing facts on various subjects. They love to store bits of information, as if their brains are file folders, which they easily and joyfully access. This is all part of the grammar stage of development.

On the other hand, during the middle school analytical stage, it's been my observation that fifth graders delight in "taking things apart," peering inside, and studying the components – whether the subjects to be dissected are machines, sentences, words, or historic events. They see each discovered part as precious and important. They break the whole into pieces, so that they can gaze upon the individual fragments, and then build stronger sentences, essays, machines, historical claims, works of art, and more.

What about high schoolers and the season of rhetoric or "constructive articulation"? One distinguishing characteristic is that many of them love to argue and debate. They thrive as they learn to use their voice and words in a powerful way to direct others toward a righteous path.

Interweaving of Subjects

To allow students to delve more deeply into their academic studies, Classical Education seeks to interweave subject areas whenever possible. The purpose is to enhance both the understanding and appreciation of the content. For example, if a student is studying ancient Rome, literature from or about ancient Rome is read. At the same time, they might also learn how Rome developed a new system of roads and invented the calendar!

The interweaving of subject areas gives students a knowledge bank that makes sense and leads to further exploration or even the launching of their own creative ideas. This is in contrast to being taught unrelated topics. I feel for our children when we say in the same school day, "Let's look at ancient Egypt, then we're going to read a Shakespearean sonnet, followed by an introduction to the great American inventor, Thomas Edison!"

Indications of Success

Two good indications that a child has learned the material presented are:

(1) They can write about what they have learned; and

(2) They can speak about the topic in a confident, intelligent manner.

Mastery

Mastery is another indication of success. In this fast-paced world, where boxes seem to cry out to be checked, this concept seems to have been lost. A child's individual expression of his understanding of what's been taught, and her ability to apply this knowledge in some way, are good indications of mastery. Teachers find rest, in knowing that their students have understood, practiced, and applied concepts, rather than in simply having all the boxes checked.

Thus, the pace set by the teacher considers the child. The homeschool Mom brings the gift of learning to the child as he/she is ready to receive it.

I encourage you, dear homeschool mother, to consider the gift of a Classical Education, literally classical rivers of blessing to be poured out on your children. I also encourage you to learn alongside them.

Many homeschooling mothers have found the best education they received was not from their own "schooling," but the one imparted to them as they taught and learned alongside their children. I certainly have experienced personal growth through various components of Classical Education as I've studied alongside my children. And I continue to grow and learn with them.

God Bless,
Michelle

12: Love of a Living Education (I)

Dear Homeschool Mom:

We have chatted about prayer and the important elements in inspiring your children, we have pondered the joy of community, and we have discussed the depth of a Classical Education. This next educational component—what I refer to as a Living Education-- makes your homeschooling SING... it makes it come ALIVE. And, isn't this what you want for your children, a living, joy-filled education?

For me, two additional ingredients are essential if you want to make any curriculum come alive. The first ingredient is what I call living food (life-giving books, inspiring people, engaging situations, and involvement in service to others). The second element is balance, which I discuss in the next chapter.

Living Books

Living books can expose our children to so many worthwhile ideas, bringing understanding and the light of wise counsel. Simply put, living books, to me, are inspirational works, written by a single author. This does not indicate that textbooks are not good – they are indeed necessary! But I have found that delving into one good book by a single author often brings the richest rewards.

The advantage to exploring this type of literature is that the reader, to some degree, lives the words of the author – as his/her perspective, heart, and soul are revealed – whether through fiction or the writer's treatment of a certain topic. It truly is amazing to be able to see through their eyes, hear through their ears, and grasp the author's unique understanding, insight, wisdom, and experience.

This is most clearly seen in the writings of the saints. Saint Thomas Aquinas takes the reader on a journey with him, climbing to new spiritual heights and seeing what he sees from an enlightened viewpoint. Saint Faustina's writings about her trust in Jesus cannot help but encourage the reader to seek this kind of intimacy with our Lord. And, as one even skims the surface of the vast writings of Saint Pope John Paul II, student and seeker alike can only stand in awe of all that he discerned and accomplished. Indeed, in reading his words of wisdom, we walk in his steps. Many will attest to having a "relationship" with the saint whose writings they have just studied. They will ask for the saint's intercession and aid in their trials, and also imitate his/her virtue and way of life.

Novels also clearly convey a message from the author as characters are developed and the reader observes or even identifies with their life choices. The path chosen may convey a message about what is most important in life. Further, books filled with photographs share both the photographer's devotion to their craft and a love of the subject matter caught on camera. Art books convey the fragility or strength of a subject. Books can be sources of inspiring quotes or words that just seem to paint a realistic picture; they can be messages that deliver like a spearhead or conveyers of thoughtful, gentle wisdom. Books written by single authors are simply living and life-giving!

Inspiring People

As homeschoolers, we have the gift of planning and preparing what we want our children to learn. We can place our homeschoolers around inspiring people who are able to have a profound and positive impact upon them, as well as create lasting memories.

God created each of us in His image and likeness. Scripture says: "in the image and likeness of God, he created them" (Genesis 1:27). This significant verse can be understood to mean that each of us reflects God in a unique and irreplaceable way. Like a little crystal vase, the image of Christ shines forth brightly from each soul. We can glean much from the light that shines forth from the hearts of others. We learn of the unique movement of God in each individual life. We learn of another's distinct creative gifts, talents, charisms, and strengths. We are exposed to their distinct personalities and forms of expression.

It is a desire of my heart to allow my children to see such bright lights. And what has surprised me is that the best and brightest lights for our family are often right at our fingertips – in the community in which we live – only waiting to be uncovered. We rarely have to go far to discover amazing stories, talents, and vision.

I find that God often places wonderful inspiring examples of faith, art, motivation, encouragement, skill, or talent right in our midst. In our family, we have been especially blessed to have living "saints" among us who inspire our children to holiness and virtue. We have met these wonderful individuals at daily Mass and on retreats. They have seen their pastor's compassionate heart, heard many "grandparents" share their stories of faith, and met holy people, as well as those "who knew holy people" (like Mother Angelica, Mother Teresa, or Padre Pio).

They have come across talented musicians in our community who have shared their musical journey and talent with our children and encouraged them in these gifts. Artists, too, have come forward and shared the ways their creativity has blessed others.

These encounters have evolved to the point that some of these special people are now such good family friends that I consider them part of our family. We cherish the time we can spend together around a meal or other get together. We have truly been blessed, and I can only hope they have been similarly enriched.

My job has been to be open and available when these "divine appointments" arise and to see them as a gift from God. This can be a challenge at times with children in tow, but I try to recognize this prompting of the Holy Spirit and respond with eagerness and expectation.

I encourage you, as a homeschool mother, to be on the lookout for people who would be a delight to your children, given their own particular interests and "bents." Invite these individuals over for lunch or dinner or meet them for coffee. It will be time well spent for all of you.

Engaging Situations

Our family loves field trips…. well, the kids love field trips! In truth, sometimes these endeavors are a lot of work. And we always seem to leave something behind – a shoe, a stuffed animal, or a snack!

However, there is no better classroom than the outdoor world, which God has created for our enjoyment. We learn so much about how "all things work for good" (Romans 8:28). Every part of nature seems to be important and play a unique role. Nothing can compare to the freedom and joy of romping through the woods, picnicking on a rock, or listening to a waterfall. This living classroom beckons and always delivers!

We also love museums. Time spent learning about a region's historical past is a rewarding investment. Museum displays and exhibits offer incredible opportunities to explore so many subject areas. Children are invited to immerse themselves in the Civil War era, dive into science and technology, or seek answers to puzzles. Museums offer endless environments for this type of expeditionary learning. As a family, we return time and again to these beautiful creative centers of learning and inquiry, and we always discover something new.

I encourage you to plan some of these kinds of field trips with your children. They will simply relish these experiences and learn and grow in new ways. Also, as field trip days seem to be the times when everything that can go wrong – and you forget at least one shoe – persevere… you will be glad you did!

Service

One more thing I wish to communicate to my family is that "the earth is not our home." Our home is heaven and our hearts must be zealously striving for all things of God.

It has been important as a family for us to participate in various service opportunities, as time allows and as we are able. We have had garage sales to raise money for the poor, helped pack food boxes, volunteered at thrift stores, and participated in other service. When we need to turn our hearts toward serving others, we can write letters to prisoners or donate clothes to our local thrift store. I want my children's minds and hearts to be firmly focused on making the world a better place one step at a time. I believe that they already are doing this, in numerous rewarding ways.

I encourage you, dear mother, not to be afraid to allow your children to bless others through service. Use creativity and initiate small actions… a two-sentence letter to an elderly friend can makes a world of difference. Let your love cast out all fear, and do not be afraid to be the light.

Living well as a homeschooling family should include bringing life experiences into our children's hearts. It is time well spent and makes homeschooling an exciting adventure.

God Bless,
Michelle

13: Love of a Living Education (II): Holy Balance

Dear Homeschooling Mom:

It is my perception that one of the greatest challenges to homeschool mothers is in finding the right balance in every area. Without this critical seesaw stability, homeschool life can become either oppressive or totally lacking in structure. Too much or too little freedom can tip the scale in the wrong direction, and this juggling act can become a real struggle. But with balance, the homeschool mother is able to work for good, as Scripture says: "We know that all things work for good for those who love God, who are called according to his purpose" (Romans 8:28).

Baking Bread

Let me explain. I like to compare homeschooling to baking bread. Bakers will readily agree that bread baking is an art. It is a culinary skill that must be studied, practiced, and perfected.

Baking requires sifting and mixing different ingredients in a certain, precise order. And these components aren't always run of the mill! Experienced bakers can be finicky about the right type of flour or the exact amount of salt. Measure and sequence are necessary. The yeast must be added to warm water before being combined with any egg mixture; it will only ferment at an optimum temperature. Each step is essential. Flour must be mixed with salt before the liquids of water/milk are added. Finally, an overall sense of what constitutes success, of what freshly baked bread should smell, taste, and look like, will help a baker tweak the recipe – and make changes as needed.

In a way similar to baking, "ingredients," steps, proportions, and order are also needed for an ideal outcome in homeschooling. A homeschooling mother selects the best components for her children and family. Sometimes a math curriculum fits one particular child; other times she chooses a history curriculum that can be adapted for several grades for multiple children. And, the day's routine can be a recipe for success or failure. Homeschooling mothers need to make deliberate decisions about the right amount of time to devote to certain subjects – too much and the kids may "protest," too little and the "ingredients" might never come together. Order is important as well: work first, then the morning break or time outdoors or lunch.

I encourage you, dear mother, to also prioritize subjects of study. Observe your children individually and as a little group. Evaluate the learning materials you are considering to see if they are a good match for a particular child.

Also, be aware of distractions. At times, children love to distract us with a favorite subject, and I have lost more than one day chasing butterflies. While these are memories I cherish, I have learned to gently redirect them back toward the tasks at hand, sooner rather than later. Allowing our students to "see and savor" and then moving on achieves a desired balance.

Object of Our Focus

Perhaps balance is really a call for a deeper focus and understanding. For this deeper kind of centeredness, we must prayerfully look at each of our child(ren) and our family as a whole. What do we desire for our children in terms of their own blossoming? Who do we hope they will become? What do we want our little domestic church to look like?

The following black and white photograph shows great balance. In the upper right section, a chair is balanced on a ladder. The man is able to accomplish this feat not because he is looking at the "balancing" act or the ladder, but because he is focusing on the CHAIR. His attention is focused squarely on the position of the chair – whether it needs to be a little more to the right or the left.

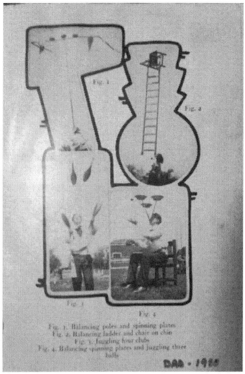

Figure 1: Aull Family pictures (1930) Josef Stullac, the man in the picture, is quoted as saying You can accomplish anything you want in life if you really want it badly enough

In a similar way, the homeschool parent successfully balances a myriad of factors. She does so successfully not because she is focused on the elements that need juggling – the soccer team or the history book – but because she understands that the child (and family) needs a bit more of this, or a little less of that. The parents are focusing on the (CHILD)REN and the FAMILY. Just as the man moves the chair a little to the right or left as needed, so too does the homeschooling mother make slight adjustments to care for her children and bring needed balance.

Also, regarding the image of the chair, it is interesting to note that it is never perfectly balanced. It always needs to be shifted slightly in one direction or another. Note, too, that the higher the chair is, the more singular the focus and the more delicate the correction. When it's most elevated, even the slightest movement to the right or the left causes a significant shift. A little change to the right or the left can remedy the situation quickly – or just as suddenly cause a fall.

Similarly, homeschool mothers, children and families are never completely balanced – that should be an encouragement to us all! We are simply called to be aware of and attentive to our children's and family's needs and to respond accordingly. Appropriate shifts, no matter how small, are advised, when and where needed!

Make no mistake: getting the chair up in the air (or beginning on the road to homeschooling in the case of a homeschool mother) is the most difficult part in the whole process. It takes a huge leap of faith, a "calling higher" for many of us. After taking that initial step, the balancing act just requires adjustments here and there – with practice, practice, practice, some falls, and always some new beginnings. Those changes in direction become easier once you know the road. It's that first step of faith that begins the homeschooling journey, and like balancing a chair on a ladder, what may seem impossible actually turns out to be surprisingly doable.

To return for a moment to the illustration of bread baking, Jesus in the Parable of the Yeast teaches, "To what shall I compare the kingdom of God? It is like yeast that a woman took and mixed (in) with three measures of wheat flour until the whole batch of dough was leavened" (Luke: 13:20-21). As homeschool moms, we can look forward to that growth and transformation in the lives of our children over time with measured amounts of select ingredients.

Finally, balance requires a sensitivity to the child's needs and heart. A mother is the most aware of the smallest directional changes, and these slight shifts often signal a movement of the Holy Spirit – or a potential problem. As mothers, we are instinctively aware of these fluctuations, and our motherly spirit can direct – or in many cases redirect – the child or family. Thus, with the Lord's leading we are able to either encourage steps forward or discourage a flight in an unwise direction.

Learning from Other Homeschooling Families

In the beginning of my own journey, I was blessed to encounter so many different homeschooling families. Much can be learned from these encounters, whether planned or seemingly by coincidence. You may glean information on the style of homeschooling that another mother has chosen, or the particular subjects being taught; you may discover certain materials that work well, or an order and rhythm of a particular homeschool family's days. One may come away with a sense of "Wow, that social studies approach or math curriculum or drama website really has something to offer." You might feel excited to pursue some of the ideas presented, or come away even more certain that, "No, that's not something I want in my home learning environment."

In my experience, God often brings together mothers whose children have similar interests or compatible temperaments. When we share our experiences as we walk this homeschool path, we can glean from one another and come away inspired. We may gain a new perspective on what works for a particular personality or temperament, grade level, or sibling age group.

I learned very quickly what was likely to succeed in our family and what probably would not. Some of these other homeschool moms inspired me to be better—in organizing (yikes), planning, and cultivating. I saw so much beauty in these friends and acquaintances, parents and children, that I could not help but implement some of their ideas and thoughts into our own family. I still do.

Being involved in a community has also allowed me to be surrounded by many children, some of whom are similar to my own in various ways. In these situations, I ask questions of the parents: what have you found that works best at this level for that subject; or where would you go to pursue a talent or interest our children seem to share? Often, just a little nudge here and there is all that is needed to strike out on a new adventure – one that may truly bless one or all of your children.

I encourage you, dear mother, to spend time asking two questions: (1) What or who will this child become?; (2) What or who is our family meant to be? In other words, what are God's plans for our children and for us all?

Obviously, we walk with God, and entrust him with the future for ourselves, our spouses, and our children. But these are questions worth asking and praying about.

God Bless,
Michelle

14: Love of Creating a Living Home

Dear Homeschooling Mom:

In the center of the body is the heart; this beating, life-giving organ has a tremendous job. It must continually supply all the oxygen that the body needs to thrive. A healthy heart is crucial to a healthy body, and an unhealthy heart can be an obstacle. We want our hearts to be healthy.

Likewise, the home is the center of a family's life. It, too, should be healthy and humming along. We want our homes to be living, thriving, and inspiring environments. And, we want our home life to run well, so that our family can be stable with a healthy pulse, able to plant and grow in different seasons, and ready to radiate this homegrown sunshine to others on chosen paths, as needed.

In many ways, the mother is the center of family life. While the father is the spiritual head, the mother ensures that life proceeds with a certain calm and constant rhythm. It is her heart that must constantly tend to myriad needs – a call to inspire and encourage. Often, her responsibilities include planning, maintaining, and nurturing all that is worthy within the home. She cultivates the good and weeds out the bad. It is a tremendous responsibility, and, of course, can only be done with the grace of the Lord.

Hallmarks of a Healthy Home

For me, a healthy home is like a heart that beats with a "happy humming heartbeat." It beats neither too fast nor too slow – it happily hums along. Now and then it can beat faster for certain short periods of time, but that is not its normal rhythm. If it beats too fast for too long, it wears itself out, as well as the body. The pace can be slowed for a while (and I do love naps), but again if it beats too slow for too long, a lackluster tiredness can set in. A healthy home, like a healthy heart, must beat rhythmically with a certain life-giving pattern to be most effective.

We know what an "unhealthy home" looks like. Most likely we've all been there – not at someone else's home, but tired, spent, exhausted, and cranky in our own domain. Housework and teaching have piled up, we have stretched ourselves beyond what was expected or realistic, and we have and even wasted precious hours on social media platforms. Our fatigue and irritability take their toll on our husband and children. They suffer in not having the things they need. Promises are not kept, and sometimes it feels as if the whole family is suffering from battle fatigue – as if our ship has sunk. Alas, this is not the little haven we wanted to create.

While God does stretch us, He also desires us to act with wisdom. Wisdom cares for her children and provides for them as she loves them. There is great wisdom in desiring to be a loving mother, and the journey to that goal requires godly wisdom.

Abode of God

Recently, our family journeyed to the Shrine of the Most Blessed Sacrament in Alabama. It was built in many ways through the outpouring of the love Mother Angelica had for the Blessed Sacrament. Everything on the grounds gives attention and reverence to the Most Blessed Sacrament.

Before our family left (on Father's Day), my husband, Chris, remarked "Wow, God sure does love this place." We sensed that God the Father was pouring out His many graces in this holy place – that He was dwelling there.

The little world of the Shrine of the Blessed Sacrament that Mother Angelica helped build exudes such excellence, reverence, beauty, and awe. Every detail – the marble, the artwork, the stained-glass windows – was obviously selected and crafted with great skill and loving care.

Before we left, I realized that I wanted much of what the shrine offers, and I felt a call to bring peace and unity, excellence and beauty into our own home. In a sense, the shrine is an "Abode of God." And while our home is not blessed with the Eucharist, my heart still wants it to be "an Abode of God" – a little footstool of His where the Lord can rest and dwell. As with what I had experienced at the shrine, I wanted our home to be a place where we might gaze upon the beautiful and the inspiring, explore bountiful collections of books, enjoy meaningful decorations, and work and rest in well thought-out spaces. What I most wanted in our home was peace and unity with the Lord's Heart.

This led to a prayer which I wrote entitled "The Abode of God" in which I asked the Lord to make our home His. (This prayer can be found in the appendix.) And while our home is far from perfectly illustrating the words in the prayer, neither was Mother Angelica's home complete for many years. With prayer and focus, we are one step closer, and this is encouraging.

A Home Full of Life

As I ponder Scripture and the story of creation, I am continually amazed at the wisdom of God. While He is the supreme Creator, our Almighty God is also a cultivator – one might even say a "farmer." In His Almighty wisdom, God spoke "Let there be light and there was light" (Genesis 1:3).

God continued creating, unfolding, and cultivating His plan, and "God saw that it was good" (Genesis 1:10, 12, 21).

As homemakers, we can likewise imitate our Creator in His work of cultivation. We can take what little we have, nurture it, and bring forth new forms of beauty and utility. The little rooms of our home can be cultivated together into a safe haven; the air in our houses can be filled with pleasing smells and sounds. Our table can beckon family and friends with delicious food and drink, as well as conversation and laughter. Our family room with a simple sofa can be transformed into a welcoming space for family prayer, sharing of talents, and entertainment. Our entryway can greet guests, both new acquaintances and old friends, with inspiring words, images, and gifts. Our bedrooms can be filled with decor that inspires calm, rest, reflection, and creativity. Life can abound in our homes. We can take what "little" seeds we have been given, cultivate them with the Lord, and reap a harvest for our families: life will abound, our souls will grow, and God will be glorified.

Dear Homeschool Mother,

While creating a living home is not something that is necessarily found in a textbook, it is one of the most important lessons that we teach our children, especially our daughters. They learn from our example of caring for all that has been entrusted to us in an ordered and nurturing way.

Whether our children grow up to manage a doctor's office, a farm, a home and family, or some combination thereof, they will know what it is to work diligently, lovingly, and gently. They will have experienced the rewards of a living environment where they and others can thrive. They themselves will not only become the first fruit, the living examples of such a home, but they will similarly plant and nurture, as they model this God-inspired "way" to the next generation. I pray that you will be inspired to create a beautiful "living home" for all to enjoy.

God Bless,
Michelle

15: Love of the Church

Dear Homeschool Mom:

Our Catholic Church is filled with tremendous graces. Being with others in a place of worship is absolutely awe inspiring – whether it's 100 gathered in a chapel, 1,000 attending Mass in a basilica or cathedral, or even 10,000 teens coming together at a global youth event with the pope.

Our Catholic Church is large, abundant, beautiful, and devout. It is also filled with graces that I want my children to experience and come to love. I want them to know that they are part of a faith that is at once personal, as well as deep, vast, and triumphant. They belong to a bigger Church community, in fact, an enormous universal Church, fulfilling its mission to bring the Gospel of Christ to every living creature.

Large Celebrations

Daily and weekly Masses at our church give my children a sense of God's glory. How wonderful it is to see so many people come together in one place, worshipping Jesus with music and a sense of reverence. One can sense the unity of spirit as those assembled grow quiet and are formed into "one body in Christ" during that precious hour of devotion, prayer, and worship.

Even as I now reflect on this, it strikes me as miraculous that individuals of different ages, from various backgrounds, locations, and walks of life can come together in worship, and emerge in unity and faith, being of one heart and voice. To ponder the enormity of such a large celebration and the memories that such occasions can create for our children, we might reflect on January, 2015, when over 6 million faithful gathered for Mass in Manila in Rizal Park as part of Pope Francis's apostolic and state celebration in the Philippines!

The Eucharistic Congress and Catechism conventions are also awe inspiring. As many as 30,000 faithful Catholics gather to give glory to God with a focus on the Eucharist, and 10,000 Catechists come to celebrate and grow in Church teaching. How can events, such as these, not give children a deeper sense of purpose and belonging? Jesus reigns and is so present at these events.

Catholic Institutions of Excellence

As a family, we make it a point to visit Catholic institutions of excellence. Being Notre Dame alumni our family has occasionally visited this magnificent university campus. It is a place where one's gaze and attention are drawn in every direction to beauty and wonders that overflow with history, teaching, and spiritual depths. Loveliness and excellence are so present in every arena from the splendid architecture of the buildings to the brilliant teaching from outstanding faculty.

So often, as in the case with Notre Dame, these places of Catholic excellence have a "back story" – a narrative in which God's guidance and grace are interwoven with the institution's historical growth. As we learn of these beginnings, we see how God directed, provided, and intervened profoundly. Sometimes saints are associated with these places.

In the example of Notre Dame, Father Basil Morreau (now Blessed) directed Father Edward Sorin to found Notre Dame in 1842. Unfortunately, just thirty-seven years later, the school building burned to the ground. With it, came the collapse of the (one-ton) white dome, encompassing the statue of Mary! Notre Dame archives contain the words of Father Sorin, as he emerged on campus four days after the fire. Walking through the ruins, he could feel the emotional devastation of the community. With that, he signaled to everyone to enter the church, where he stood on the altar steps and spoke these words:

> If it were all gone, I should not give up. I came here as a young man and dreamed of building a great university in honor of Our Lady. But I built it too small, and she had to burn it to the ground to make the point. So, tomorrow, as soon as the bricks cool, we will rebuild it, bigger and better than ever. (https://175.nd.edu/175-moments/the-great-fire/)

The Notre Dame website further states "They rebuilt it from the ground up, and when they got to the top, and came to the place where the dome had been, they built one taller and wider than the one before. This one (Statue of Mary) would be covered in gold."

Father Sorin was undeterred, and another larger school building was built and opened the following school year. As expressed in his quote, the original building was simply not big enough.

Another remarkable example of an institution of excellence is Boy's Town in Omaha, Nebraska. Father Edward Flanagan, the community's founder, built an entire city on the property for the express purpose of taking in "troubled youth." His biography recalls a comment, made by a boy, literally carrying another younger resident: "He is not heavy, he is my brother."

We can recall Mother Angelica, the founder of EWTN, a "cloistered nun" who took a "field trip" by accident to a television studio "up North." There, she saw the power of a satellite dish and said that she had to have one for Jesus. Thus, she ordered one. Months later the satellite arrived by way of a company representative who expected to be paid $600,000 upon delivery. As she didn't have the money, Mother Angelica went into the chapel, knelt before Jesus, and said "Jesus, your satellite dish has arrived." Moments later, a nun entered the same chapel, announcing that a donor was on the phone offering to give EWTN $600,000! (https://wbhm.org/feature/2016/mother-angelica-and-the-eternal-word-television-network/)

We also can peek into untold numbers of monasteries, cathedrals, shrines, missions, pro-life centers, and even hospitals to find the lives and stories of saints and blessed souls interwoven into the foundation and fabric of these holy places. These sacred places offer so much to absorb – excellence, passion, devotion, and a tirelessness in proclaiming the Good News of the Gospel.

The Church is One

While studying abroad, it was always a wonder to me that while attending Mass, though it was spoken in a different language, I still could participate in the celebration and be very blessed. Liturgy has a flow that remains constant and consistent in any and every language. At the same time, the culture of a given location gives the liturgy a certain flavor. While not being able to understand the homily, it was still miraculous to be able to join in the Our Father and take in the expressions of the local ethnic culture brought to life through song, prayer, and dress.

The Holy Rosary

It always lifts my soul to pray the rosary in a large group. It seems to me that our Blessed Mother has gathered together an army in these times in which we are living. There is nothing like 1,000 voices united in saying the rosary, marching together as little soldiers for Mary. To be united in prayer in this way brings peace, harmony, and a presence of calmness through repetition. Saint Louis De Montford wrote, "that when one person prays the rosary individually, he gains the merit of one rosary, whereas a person who recites the rosary in the group gains merit for all the rosaries prayed by each person." (*The Secret of the Rosary*: https://www.montfort.org.uk/Writings/ASR.php)

I encourage you, dear homeschool mother, to make time to take advantage of these blessings, thereby giving strength to your children and to yourself as well.

God Bless,
Michelle

16: Love of the Cross (I): Authenticity

Dear Homeschool Mom:

My husband wisely suggested that I not gloss over some of the "sweat and tears" of homeschooling. Yes, quite simply, it is hard work, not occasionally, but constantly. A Catholic pastor once told me that one of the most difficult challenges of the priesthood is living and working in the same place. He shared that there is really no separation between the church and the rectory (the supposed place of rest); thus, it is a vocation of almost constant work. Sacraments must be administered at various times to save souls; the phone rings with people in crisis at all hours, or, depending on the parish, they may even show up unannounced at the front door. The priest is always "on duty."

In some ways, homeschooling is like this. Home also is the "place" where our children's souls are most formed, and ours as well. It can be especially trying to "work out my own salvation," while guiding my child to do the same.

Bad Days Do Happen

Some days are just rough. One of my children may wake up cranky, while another has his mind set on a single objective that does not really fit into the day's plan. Perhaps a third child just won't get out of bed! Still, we begin. But, the math concepts are not being understood, or a sibling fight breaks out over who has done the most work that morning! A particular homeschool book has disappeared; the work that was done yesterday is nowhere to be found; even the simplest of tools, our pencils, seem to have been misplaced. Learning, what learning? The task of homeschooling even one of my children, let alone all of them seems unexpectedly overwhelming.

As I reflect on these moments, I realize that I have let my gaze slip from the love and power of our Almighty God to the problems at hand… and, with that shift, down I go. I begin to create a mountain out of the day's issues, and every minute, these concerns seem to get bigger and bigger. My mind is cluttered, alternating from "tailspin" mode to just plain weariness.

I begin to slide from my role of nurturing and teaching to that of "traffic director," fearful the day will unravel with little accomplished. About this time, I recognize that I have become the grumpy one – out of sorts because my day isn't going as scheduled. Now, we're all in trouble! At the whirlpool of cross currents, I even find myself inviting the family to jump into this vortex with me.

And we all know the saying… If Momma isn't happy, no one is happy.

And, so begins a bad day… a start that hopefully will be short-lived.

However, I need not fear – I am not alone! God is present with me in these moments. As I turn my gaze toward Him and seek His will, He will direct my steps. There may need to be some quiet time for everyone, a walk, or a time to all sit together and ask God to help us in this moment! Most often, what is called for is an apology from Mommy. When I turn to Him with sincerity, He never fails to guide me, teach me, and provide what is needed.

I have also found (humorously) that when one of my kids is in really big trouble, that is precisely the moment that Grandma shows up on our doorstep – with a welcome surprise. I may have wanted this child to learn a lesson the hard way (due to my unforgiveness), but obviously God had other plans. Thus, we all enjoy the brownies or cookies my own mother has come bearing. Saved by Grandma!

Carrying the Cross as a Mother

A homeschool mother's heart desires to inspire her children with all that is best for them and most beautiful. Oh, how she suffers as she seeks to bring these graces to her children. Many homeschool mothers will attest to significant conflict with family and friends, not to mention the children themselves – all while saying firmly but gently "no, this is what is best at this time." It happens gradually and slowly, even through many battles. Yet, in time, her children learn to love what her heart loves, to see what her eyes see, and eventually to accept the very cross of Christ themselves. Her heart has directed them toward Jesus and the cross, and has taught them the love of the cross – the love of suffering for another with the hope for their greater good.

At each stage in a child's growth, they are given tremendous gifts that they can observe, embrace, and eventually steward wisely. Toddlers are given the power to walk, but this forward movement comes with many falls. An ever-watchful mother is quickly by their side to scoop them up. At age two or three, children find their voice – NO – but they must be taught to use this vocal gift to build and bless, and this comes only after many times of correction. Perhaps the most painful learning occurs at the onset of adulthood, when our children begin to walk in the gift of free will more fully. They are now able to make their own choices, and with that bear the blessings and burdens of their decisions.

Mothers, in particular, can suffer terribly when children spread their wings and fly – sometimes right into a wall. This can cause tremendous suffering as a mother can see, like no one else, the beauty and potential of each of her children. They are unconditionally beautiful in her eyes! But they still make unwise and silly choices at times, and this stretches her heart in prayer and expectant hope.

However, as mothers, we, too, are given a tremendous gift – that of knowing we can turn to the Lord in deep prayer with expectant faith for our children. We can trust that the Lord is God and He has unique plans for each of our children. He uses our prayers to bless our children in the most perfect and abundant ways to draw them closer to Himself.

I have seen in my own life amazing answers to these heartfelt prayers. Saints intervene and intercede as novenas are prayed, and Mother Mary holds tremendous "sway" with her Son. In my own life, God has moved powerfully; He has moved just as mightily in my children's hearts. This is a testament to His Almighty grace and power. I have no doubt that He will continue to work in their lives, and in mine, as I bring my desires, needs, and concerns to Him.

However, I am learning that for the Lord to truly fill me with prayer and expectant hope, I must be empty of worry and anxiety. These fears and emotions cannot fill my vessel; rather, I must allow the Lord to saturate me with His love.

Being Filled with Forgiveness

Perhaps more than with any other vocation, the job of being a homeschool mother requires forgiveness. This is not because it is a source of deep wounds (although sometimes this is so), but because repeated offenses seem to be part of the homeschool landscape. Homeschool mothers must forgive. They must forgive often and they must forgive much. We forgive because of the love we have for our children, and because we are willing to patiently teach them – once again the same lesson, perhaps from a different angle, only a little deeper, a little higher.

For me, the cross can be summed up with Jesus's words on the cross. "Father, forgive them for they know not what they do" (Luke 23:34). Who is the person who "knows NOT what they do"?? Who can that person be, other than a CHILD, who does not know, who needs gentle direction and instruction? Even if the challenging person is an adult, from the right perspective he or she can and should be seen as a "child," who in Jesus's mind has a future and a hope. In both cases, a child who is being showered with forgiveness is being called "higher."

When conflict or obstacles do arise in this endeavor, we will continue to forgive, to patiently teach and guide following the words of Jesus: "Father forgive them for they know not what they do."

Redemptive Suffering

I once read that one of the biggest losses to humanity has been the loss of the spiritual practice of uniting the pain we have in this life to the cross – and transforming it into redemptive suffering. Redemptive suffering has infinite and eternal value. It is a river of grace. However, I am not sure that many of us know what redemptive suffering is or what redemptive suffering looks like. It is a process and a path (through prayer), as we unite ourselves to Christ and reflect upon His journey.

In prayer, the Lord is having me create steps… little stepping stones for me to stand on … to travel on … as I am guided around the "mountain" of any suffering in my life. I will share these eight steps, in hopes that they will bless you in your walk with Him, as you pass through valleys and various trials and tribulations.

Step #1: Identify the pain and suffering. I believe God does not cause pain, although He has given us the ability to FEEL pain. This ABILITY to feel pain, not the pain itself, is a gift from God. It is an indication that something is wrong. If we did not feel pain, we would not know that there was "an injury." In the physical world, I can easily bleed if I do not take care of a large cut. In the spiritual world I also need to identify the pain I am feeling – rejection, hurt, being ignored, whatever it is at the time. The more that I can identify the different types of pain I am feeling – physical, spiritual, emotional – the degree of pain, and the cause, such as emotional heartache with family or friends, the more I am able to present it to the Lord for His help and healing.

Step #2: Place the pain and suffering into His loving hands. In doing so, I am able to see that His hands are loving and gentle and His face is full of kindness. I am able to gaze on the face of my Savior, Jesus the Christ, who KNOWS and understands. I trust Him with the cross that I am carrying when I surrender my suffering into His care.

Step #3: Find the suffering I am experiencing in the Passion of Jesus. This simply can be done by asking the question: "Where and when did Jesus feel this pain?" We believe that Jesus on the cross suffered every pain we will ever experience. If I feel lonely, I know that Jesus felt lonely on the cross. If I feel abandoned by friends, I know that Jesus felt abandoned by friends in the garden. If I feel not heard, I know that Jesus felt the same way before Pilate.

Some of the pains of a mother can often be found at the foot of the cross in Mary's heart as she suffered with her son, or earlier when she had to flee to Egypt and make her home in a foreign country for a time. Sometimes, I have found that it is easier to find the pain of a mother in Mary's heart. She knows what it feels like to see a child suffer and feel helpless to rescue him. She knows what it is to behold beauty and see it wounded.

In uniting my suffering with Christ's, I am able to walk inside His Sacred Heart, where He speaks to me of His journey. The deeper and more painful the hurt, the more embraced I feel. He wills to share His thoughts, His feelings, His actions, His desires – His prayers, indeed His Sacred Heart with me. While it may be painful in the Heart of Jesus, I have found it to be very peaceful and comforting.

Step #4: Have expectant hope. God always is doing something new. If God is allowing this pain, it is only because He wills to do a tremendous and powerful work.

Step #5: Begin to pray as Jesus prayed in His pain. **Jesus bestowed blessing upon those who were hurting Him**. "Father forgive them for they know not what they do." Then He bestowed the greatest blessings upon them: the grace to become children of God. He opened up the treasures of His heart and prayed blessings upon them, pouring out his love and mercy. You and I are able, though it may be difficult, to repeat those same words with Jesus. I do not say them by myself, He walks with me (and with you) as we say these prayers for those who have offended or wounded us.

Step #6: Continue to pray for all those who are experiencing the same pain, yet do not know how to pray. Jesus did not limit His prayer to only those who were tormenting Him. His prayer knew no bounds. My prayer must also increase to touch all those it may reach. On the cross, I believe Jesus knew that I would be experiencing the same pain, and He prayed for me at that time (though far away from Him physically and in time) to have faith in "our" Father. He knew I would be experiencing the same pain, and He prayed I would have great faith in "Our" heavenly Father. By His words "Father, forgive them…" He directs my attention toward God the Father. It is there that I find hope.

United to Jesus, and following His example, I likewise also am called to **pray for all those who are experiencing the same pain, yet do not have the faith that I may have.**

A retreat leader, Cricket Aull, OFS, once said:

> If we are going through any suffering ourselves, there is an especially important point to remember: We can use our own suffering as a prayer to God for people who are going through the same trials, but without faith. We become the prayer they need. Christ did this for us, and we grow more into Christ's love and faithfulness as we do this ourselves. Please use your suffering trials as a way to help others, as Christ used His suffering to help us and restore us to the Father's love. (From a talk titled, *Living in the present moment.*)

In their loneliness or heartache, they do not know how to talk to Jesus or even that He longs for this communication with them. It seems to me that with each and every prayer, a small candle is lit before God for all eternity.

Step #7: **Pray for all those who do not yet know the love of Jesus.** Holiness attracts, and any suffering I feel may draw others to my example. Saint Maximilian Kolbe is said to have stated, "the greatest book was the cross." Likewise, by my prayer and example, as I am united to Christ, I can become a light to others. God sometimes wills that I be inspired by the valiant life of a saint, who united himself or herself to Christ through his or her suffering. In some small way also, as ordained by God, my life, prayers, and trust may be a light to others, even as I struggle.

Step #8: Make a small act of faith in humility. Lou Holtz, the Hall of Famer (and former Notre Dame football coach) said "do the next right thing." Rather than dwelling upon the situation, I am propelled forward through a small action. Sometimes the next right thing is speaking a kind word or simply beginning the dishes. This slight movement away from the "mountain of suffering" steers me on a better path to continue my journey.

As needed, I can repeat the process in prayer and usually the heaviness is lifted for a time.

We All Have a "Mini Stigmata"

One of our favorite family saints is Padre Pio. His life was one of courage, as he lived through suffering, while fulfilling the will of God. The Lord allowed Padre Pio's unity to Him to be visibly seen through a *stigmata* – the suffering of the wounds of Christ. His stigmata was visible in the bleeding wounds of his hands and feet, which were united to Jesus in suffering.

I wonder if we all don't have a "stigmata," a visible (or invisible) painful wound where the Lord's will is fulfilled in us simply by grace. One mother may carry a heavy cross of raising ten children, united to Christ as she answers this high calling; for another the cross is physical suffering; for so many others it is persecution. Did Jesus not suffer physical suffering, carry a heavy cross, and endure persecution? Are these not as visible as a stigmata? Do they not have the potential to be as holy and as powerful instruments of His grace?

Know, dear homeschool mom, that the cross you carry is seen by God, and that He suffers in seeing you suffer. How pleased He is with your courageous efforts. May you know how deeply His Heart reaches out to you with mercy and compassion. May you also know how steadfast His faith and trust is in you.

God Bless,

Michelle

17: Love of the Cross (II): Brokenness

Dear Homeschooling Mom

Every life is a journey, and on this journey the soul will find that her path intertwines at times with Jesus, in His Passion and suffering.

Just as the Lord wishes to share with us great joys, it is natural that He desires also to share His sorrow and suffering. Friends share their hearts with each other, and the depth of this sharing can be an indication of the depth of their friendship.

So it should not surprise those of us who desires to walk closely with Jesus, that pain, suffering, and sorrow cross our individual paths, not as something to be feared, but rather to be embraced. This identification with the sorrows of others is what we experience in the most honest and loving of friendships.

Because mothers possess amazingly creative hearts, it should not surprise us that certain elements at the core of our being (or that which we've created) sometimes break and fall apart. I believe this is part of the natural journey of motherhood, and even more so, of homeschooling.

There was a time in my own life when my whole being seemed broken into thousands of pieces. During this season, I could only look at the shattered glass lying all around me. It seemed there was nothing I could do to put the pieces back together – like broken glass, no glue could mold those fragments into their former shape. I could have cried for a month – it was that difficult a time.

Perhaps the hardest part was the seeming silence from heaven. I could not understand what God was doing in this situation or how I was supposed to grow from it. The word I kept hearing was TRUST. And trust, I learned, is a difficult path to tread.

As I walked though this darkness and sat amid the fragments, life went on. God led me to understand that I was to take one piece of the shattered glass, hold it, pray over it, and watch to see what would happen.

I began to daily take one part of my life – a child's scouting event, for example – and hold it in prayer, even while I was there present. Then, I watched and waited. The fragment grew, it became bigger, and the "glass" took on a different shape. In fact, I eventually became the Committee Chair of our Scout Pack. I did this with each piece of "broken glass." They all grew and took on new and artistic forms and sizes.

It was challenging because all the ensuing activities and ministries stretched me, and this type of personal extension is painful. But in this challenging situation, this broader path clearly was the best to follow. In fact, I overextended myself a bit, to be honest. But I tried to be a servant and fill in the gaps I saw and experienced, as needed.

As all these individual pieces grew, the time came when I could actually put the broken fragments together again. What I found was that the shape of this new "vase" looked entirely different from the original. It was no longer tall and slim, but was instead fat and round. *The Lord had enlarged my heart to a place where it could hold so much more than seemed possible before these trials.* I stood back amazed at what God had accomplished in the darkness without my knowledge. I was unaware that I was being formed anew. I believe it was that innocent ignorance that allowed Him to achieve this transformation in me. Had I realized what was taking place, I probably would have interfered with His creative, life-giving work.

Wisdom from the Broken Road

As I traveled down this broken road, I found few resources (in the earthly realm) to help me understand the road I was on. What I did run across only confirmed the darkness I was experiencing, without offering any insight or practical steps or shedding new light. The discoveries I made were step by step in which I trusted the Lord to guide me day by day and moment by moment.

Ultimately, I discovered a couple of lights that were helpful to me during this time of brokenness. Hopefully, these beacons can "speed up" the healing process for others who may be navigating a similar path. Sharing one's own journey makes one vulnerable, but it also allows the heart to speak to others, as they, too, are challenged with life's "crossings." This type of openness gives one a voice.

Trust

Trusting in the Lord can be difficult to put into practice. It is truly an act of faith in dark times, as we remind ourselves that "The righteous cry out, the LORD hears and he rescues them from all their afflictions" (Psalm 34:18).

Trust is like walking in the dark. One evening, during this tumultuous time, I literally went out for a walk at night – in the darkness. The Lord led me by a garden in bloom – I knew the flowers were there, but in the darkness, I could not make out the lovely hues and other details. The Lord spoke to my heart saying, "Both the flowers and their colors are present, but you can only see the flowers now, because it is night." In the same way, during what feels like a dark night of the soul, God is present, walking beside us, even if we can barely find Him.

To me, trust is a two-step process. First, I must believe that the Lord is still speaking to me. Sometimes, in difficult circumstances and trying times, or when we are faced with challenging people, it can be tempting to think that the Lord's voice or direction has changed. Saint Ignatius of Loyola warns of this in his teaching on the Discernment of Spirits. In Rule 5 of his Rules for Discernment, he wrote, "In time of desolation never to make a change; but to be firm and constant in the resolutions and determination in which one was the day preceding such desolation." (https://scepterpublishers.org/blogs/scepter-blog-corner/14-rules-for-the-discernment-of-spirits-by-st-ignatius-of-loyola)

During these times, it can be easy to doubt it is the voice of the Lord speaking to my heart giving me ideas and inspirations. While God may be encouraging me to go forward with a larger plan or even a small task, obstacles can seem to arise out of nowhere. The last time our family went on a pilgrimage, my son had an accident the day before departure and received ten staples in his leg. My heart was still excited about going on the trip, but I was unsure if I was listening to the Lord and seeking His will in this endeavor. I had to lay everything at the Lord's feet once again. Confirmation actually came from my son who said, "Mommy, I really want to go. I can do this." We went, and it was a very memorable spiritual trip, especially for my son! Clearly, the Lord was speaking, although circumstances were sending a different message. We chose to listen to the Lord.

Secondly, trust is always about believing in the character of God. God is good. God's character never changes. He is always faithful, always loving, always kind. God always wants the highest and deepest for us. His will is perfect love. Nothing comes from the Father's Heart that is not pure love for His children.

Trust Means Climbing Higher

In trust we climb higher. As I meditate upon Jesus on the cross, I sometimes think of Him as climbing a very high and difficult mountain of faith. As He takes our sins upon himself, he cries out, "My God, my God, why hast thou forsaken me?" (Matthew 27:46). These words were spoken, I believe, in the darkest and most difficult moments of His Passion. But even then, His climb was not yet finished. To create an earthly picture, I think of climbing Mt. Everest, where the final steps are the most difficult and treacherous. It was so during Jesus's Passion. But moments later, He reached the pinnacle triumphant, declaring "Father, into Your hands I commend my spirit" (Luke 23:46).

In those few minutes, nothing really changed physically; however, the Heart of Jesus grew brighter. His words went from calling out, "My God" to calling Him "Father." I do not believe this was done out of a spiritual consolation, but out of a pure act of the will. He willed to see the beauty and color and radiance of His Father, even though He could not yet "see" it. He willed to see the FATHER in the darkness. He willed to believe, to hope, to expect.

I have always believed in my heart that it was at this triumphant moment in which Jesus "received" (I don't know a better word) the grace to bestow upon us the Eucharist, instituted at the Last Supper – the source and summit of our Catholic Faith. At the highest point of the Holy Mass, indeed at the pinnacle, the priest says the words, "All glory, and honor are yours Almighty FATHER."

Perhaps this can inspire us (in our own walks) to follow Jesus's example in times of brokenness. The greatest dreams can be realized in the most difficult times. Words cannot begin to describe the amazing, creative, and restorative work that Jesus accomplished in and through His Passion. God can use our brokenness in ways that reflect this redemptive work, even when the pieces lay scattered around us. He brings not only restoration, but new creations, reflecting His handiwork. Because this is WHO God is and how He chooses to work most powerfully in His children.

Write Your own Prayer or Journey

Sister Faustina Maria Pia of the Sisters of Life wrote a beautiful prayer of trust. It is in the appendix and has helped me many times when faith and hope were needed in a given situation. She described how she wrote it during a dark time in her life when she needed to grow in trust. Truly, her prayer radiates the goodness of Jesus and her abiding faith in Him.

At one point, as I read this inspiring prayer, I realized that another prayer – my own – was rising up in my heart, and that this, too, needed to be prayed. At first, I was confused and disappointed by this knowledge. But then the Lord spoke to me and said, "Why don't you write your own prayer of trust?" And so, I did. It, too, is in the appendix. The greater gift that I received from Sister Faustina Pia was not her faith-filled prayer, though it did minister to me; rather, it was in the fact that she wrote HER OWN PRAYER of trust in a dark time, and that I was encouraged by the Lord to do the same.

I wanted God to use the faith and hope that I was placing in Him in a powerful way to move mountains in the lives of others, to do unheard of things, to build His kingdom in a mighty way. My heart wanted God to use the suffering I bore for His kingdom to build and make something beautiful. I wanted this situation to be for the glory of God and for Him alone, for His kingdom. That became my prayer.

In the depth of my heart, I believed He was a good God and a faithful Father. This was how I was led to pray. Sometimes, part of the journey is learning how to pray for the situation or person in our lives. God wants our prayers to be heartfelt because He wants to move mountains with them. What started out as a prayer of trust actually ended up as a prayer of expectation, a prayer of faith and hope.

Of the three theological virtues – faith, hope, and love – love is definitely the strongest. However, hope is in the middle. Hope is the tip of the spearhead, and it pierces the enemy leading to his defeat. Hope says there will be a better day; hope says God is always doing something new.

Lessons from Saint Therese

Another piece of wisdom I have gleaned is to be thankful and to cultivate the many gifts the Lord has placed in my life. The smallest flower holds such splendor, but sometimes it is not until we are forced to slow down that we actually behold and savor its beauty, and even build upon it.

Father Jacques Phillipes in his book, *Interior Freedom*, wrote of Saint Therese:

> In the darkness we become so thankful for the littlest ray of light ….Therese lives in very wide horizons, which are those of God's infinite mercy and her unlimited desire to love him. She feels like a queen with the whole world at her feet, because she can obtain anything from God, and through love, she can travel to every point in the globe where a missionary needs her prayer and sacrifices!

He added:

> It gave me the unexpected chance of going into the enclosure of the Lisieux Carmel and discovering, with

joy and emotion, the actual places where Therese lived: the infirmary, the cloister, the laundry, the garden with the chestnut-tree avenue---all places that I knew from the saint's description of them in her autobiographical writings. One thing struck me: these places were much smaller than I could have imagined. For example, at the end of her life Therese gives a good-humored account of the sisters dropping by to have a little chat with her on their way to make hay; but the great hayfield I had pictured to myself is in reality a mere pocket-handkerchief!... However, and this is the paradox that struck me, when you read Therese's writing you never get the impression of a life spent in a restricted world, but just the opposite... There is a whole study waiting to be done on the importance of the terms by Saint Therese to express the unlimited dimensions of the spiritual universe she inhabits: "infinite horizons," "immense desires," "oceans of graces," "abysses of love," "torrents of mercy," and so on. (Scepter, 2007, pages 18-19)

An attitude of thanksgiving builds great cities and communities, and really makes a little heaven on earth. Saint Therese was indeed faithful.

Acknowledge Others are on their Own Journey
Challenges often involve a person or people who are not necessarily inclined to act the way I think is best. I have often wanted to react verbally, or otherwise, in such situations, rather than prayerfully responding or leading in love. While I sometimes have wanted to "push" these individuals toward the path that I felt would be best, I've had to remember that they are on their own journey, as I am on mine. I need to let them walk the path they choose, and trust

that God will be accompanying them, no matter how off course I think they may be.

Repent and Step Forward in Faith

One of the biggest battles I have fought in my own struggles has been in knowing that I had contributed to the shattering I spoke of earlier. Satan loves to take a tiny piece of truth and blow it out of proportion – even making it our focal point, if possible. This only builds confusion, blame, and shame, which is not from the Lord. Confusion only makes the darkness heavier and last longer. We do not want to be confused.

A better road is to recognize the small fault or wrong turn for what it is, and then to take appropriate action with patience and wisdom. Wisdom provides a path forward that is constructive and cultivates life.

Dear Mom: Yes, we all experience little episodes of the shattered glass on the floor – shattered dreams and hopes for our children, a certain curriculum, a family friendship, or a much-anticipated activity. But this is a calling that is indeed united to the Holy Spirit; and a work born out of a mother's heart. New learning materials are discovered, fresh friendships are formed, improved schedules are implemented. Because so much creativity is required in homeschooling, when something no longer fits for a child or a season, we can feel broken.

During these times, know that the Holy Spirit is always conceiving in us something new. It is wise then to refocus on our child(ren), and in prayer, grow from there.

When we can pray specifically about a situation or loss or challenge, we can grow and be prepared to build the "new" that is needed. We can trust that with the Lord's help this new direction will be even better, taking us to a higher level. Let us live the words "Be Not Afraid."

God Bless,
Michelle

18: Love of the Eucharist

Dear Homeschooling Mom:

This chapter is so intimidating to write. On the one hand, what can possibly be said that can give witness to the gift of Jesus in the Eucharist? There is not a word, a sentence, a paragraph, a book, or even a library that can begin to testify to this grace. On the other hand, how can I not share this love and joy?

If there is one thing I desire to pass along to my children, it is an understanding and a love of the Eucharist.

The Gift of the Presence

In the Eucharist, Jesus gives us the gift of His presence. Jesus is present in the Eucharist. He is the Eucharist. Quite simply, Jesus is fully present on the altar.

His Heart is present. His Kingdom is present. His wisdom is present. His family is present. His direction is present. His vision is present. His love is present. His mercy is present.

Jesus is wholly present. He is fully present. He is gloriously present. He is victoriously present. He is majestically present.

He is present as a Friend. He is present as a Shepherd. He is present as Creator. He is present as Healer. He is present as the Divine Physician.

Jesus is present as our Savior. He is present as our healer, our Divine Physician. He is present as our Teacher, our Counselor and our King.

Often, as I kneel before Him, I am amazed as Jesus touches my heart profoundly in one of these areas (as my Healer, my Shepherd, my Savior); and is present in whatever way I need Him most at that moment — often in an area where I thought I was the least needy! He is with me in a profound sense that I can only be thankful for. His "presence" and gifts are perfect and complete.

REFLECTIONS

Sometimes a bit of reflection can help one grow in one's love of the Eucharist.

Presence Before a King:

I remember being disappointed several years ago that our family could not travel to see the pope when he visited America. But the Lord directed me to make a Eucharistic visit to the Adoration Chapel at our parish. I remember Jesus encouraging me with the words: "The pilgrims have the opportunity to be in the presence of the Vicar of Christ (the pope), and that is where they need to be. I have called you to be in my presence, in my court among my angels." After reflecting on those words, how could I want to be anywhere else? To be "summoned" to a Eucharistic visit with my God, what an honor!

Full Weight:

We believe that Jesus is truly present, body, mind, soul and divinity. We do not "see" or "feel" him physically. This is a gift. Perhaps we would have difficulty receiving this gift if all our senses were opened. Can you imagine receiving Jesus, a fully grown man on your hand?

Hiddenness of Jesus:

There is such wisdom in the hiddenness of Jesus in the Eucharist. I have often pondered the hiddenness, the quietness, the stillness, the silence of Jesus present in the sacrament. He seems to be drawing me in, inviting me to be quiet, still, silent, and humble before Him. Perhaps that's because it is the direction I need to go.

Jesus Offers Himself:

We see faithfulness in the Eucharist. Jesus is so humble that He allows Himself to be called down upon an altar through one of His servants. Then He will "travel" with the priest, as the consecrated Host, into a tabernacle, into a cloth to visit the sick, on a walk to bless the people, wherever He is needed. There is no discussion, there is no committee, there is no consensus. Jesus simply makes Himself available. We see Jesus further fulfill the words from the book of Ruth, as Ruth expresses her faithfulness to her mother-in-law. "Wherever you go I will go, wherever you lodge I will lodge. Your people shall be my people" (Ruth1:16). Jesus remains faithful. Jesus remains present.

The Big Question:

The question is: "What is the difference between the grace of Jesus present in the Incarnation and the presence of Jesus in the Eucharist?"

The Answer:

The difference between these two is six feet. In the Incarnation, Jesus willed to humble Himself assuming human flesh. Our God was incarnated in human flesh. He came down. He humbled Himself. If we were to become an ant, that would pale in comparison to the humility of our God in the Incarnation.

In the Shroud of Turin (which is believed to be the covering which wrapped Jesus when He was placed in the tomb), evidence suggests that Jesus was six feet tall. So, the power of God came down from heaven and was made visible in the Incarnation of a six-foot-tall man.

In the Eucharist, Jesus builds on the Incarnation as the Son of Man. Then He descends even lower, six feet, into a small Host, a tiny piece of bread, about a millimeter high.

Perhaps Jesus "grows" the miracle of the Incarnation, or maybe one could say He adds onto the humility that was present in the Incarnation. It would seem, in a sense, that a piece of bread represents greater humility than taking on human flesh as a man. Being present as the flesh for man to eat requires greater humility than taking on the image of man himself, as true God and true man, again in a sense.

Being Present with Jesus:

At times, after I enter the sanctuary, although I have physically "arrived," it seems that I am not yet at the place where I need to be. Set before me is the challenging path to be fully present with Jesus in the tabernacle or monstrance. I must fight my way through so many distractions: the church is too hot/or cold; someone is making noise; I wonder if they are going to close the church early; am I wearing the right outfit?; how much time do I have?; is this where I am called to be now?; does a child at home need me?; did I forget to turn off the iron?; what is for dinner? There are so many battles distracting me, and in each one I must say, gently, but firmly, "Jesus you are present, redirecting my focus to what is really important: You in the Eucharist."

Through this jungle of obstacles, my heart eventually "arrives" and is able to be silent and present with Jesus. Here I bring Him the gifts I have come to offer. I bring Him honor and glory. I honor Him by saying with my life that nothing is more important than acknowledging His presence in the Eucharist. I bring Him gifts of thanksgiving and praise. Most importantly, I allow Him to guide me into silent and still worship, a place in my heart where He reigns here on earth. These are such simple gifts. They are hard fought, however, to bring to Jesus, so they must have some significance, however small.

I gently share this spiritual "pilgrimage" with my children, so they, too, can know of this journey, and bring Him gifts from their hearts, as they are led. It is a journey and I feel so blessed to be able to impart the path I have discovered with them. It is so beautiful to share our thoughts as we ponder His grace together and grow in love of this very special gift.

Eucharistic Celebration:

I believe that, as mothers, if we truly lived the liturgy of the Eucharistic Celebration, our home, our table, and our teaching would be much richer. This grace transmits our hearts to our children, our traditions, our special celebrations, and even our family culture.

I believe that He has a lot to teach me about the manner in which He celebrated the Eucharist. As mothers who regularly prepare meals and teachings, we should ponder how Jesus served His apostles at the Last Supper by reflecting upon His words and actions: most meals are not called to be a "high feast," but every meal can touch the hearts of those who partake of it.

Jesus Reveals His Own Heart:

Scripture records the great desire of Jesus: "I have eagerly desired to eat this Passover with you" (Luke 22:15). This had been a yearning in Jesus's Heart for many years. He had been preparing the minds and hearts of His disciples through His life, teachings, and miracles, so that they now are open to receiving Him in this new way and at this moment. They have come to understand that Jesus is God. "Simon Peter said, 'You are the Messiah, the Son of the Living God'" (Matthew 16:16). They remember Jesus's statement to the crowd: "I am the Bread of Life" (John 6:35). He has been leading and guiding their hearts to understand that He, God, wishes to draw so near to them in such intimate form, as to be food, food which can be consumed. This is a longing, in fact, the longing of His Sacred Heart to be at one, in union with man.

Mothers long to gather their children and families around one table so that they all may feast together. This is a mother's heart. Our meals and feasts can have significant meaning in the lives of our children. First, by their consistency and constancy, and second by the union of hearts and minds around our table (even if only for a moment).

Jesus Builds Upon Tradition:

The traditions of the Old Testament are further built upon at the Last Supper. How long had Jesus been pondering the gift of the First Eucharist? How long had He been laying the foundation, grace upon grace?

One may argue, and find Biblical evidence, that this had been the plan of God beginning with Abraham: "God Himself will provide the sheep for the burnt offering" (Genesis 22:8). Yes, grace upon grace had been added, just as love builds upon love.

In the same way, I can introduce newness in our family life from traditions already set forth, discussions previously engaged in, and memories we all share.

Jesus Prepares:

He sent two of his disciples and said to them, "Go into the city and a man will meet you, carrying a jar of water. Follow him. Wherever he enters, say to the master of the house, 'The Teacher says, "Where is my guest room where I may eat the Passover with my disciples?"' Then he will show you a large upper room furnished and ready. Make the preparations for us there." The disciples then went off, entered the city, and found it just as he had told them; and they prepared the Passover. (Mark 14: 13-16)

Here we see Jesus giving both time and thought to the planning of the Passover. Shopping needed to be done, a place needed to be arranged for, and a table needed to be set.

Likewise, a bit of planning on my end will make any gathering go more smoothly, and the meal more pleasant. Planning for the more important events of the day is time well spent. Mealtime can be a sacred time, and a little preparation can yield such delicious fruit. I know that I appreciate a nicely laid table, and I am sure my husband and children do as well.

Jesus Chooses the Best:

It would seem to me that Jesus would have chosen the best wine for the Passover. He certainly did at the Wedding at Cana. He certainly does as He chooses to give us "His blood" as our drink. Wow! Only the best.

Likewise, I, too, with a little extra foresight and love, can choose important elements to highlight in our dinner celebration, allowing those "ingredients" to shine forth. I have always felt that love can be "tasted," as can attest anyone who has compared a homemade baked item or loaf of bread to a store-bought one!

Jesus Protects and Preserves:

Throughout Jesus's ministry He was bent on protection. He states this priority in Scripture: "When I was with them I protected them in your name that you gave me, and I guarded them, and none of them was lost, except the son of destruction, in order that the Scripture might be fulfilled" (John 17:12).

My job as a homeschooling mother is to protect those entrusted to my care. It is also one of cultivation, so that they come through their journey so much richer and fuller. As wine is cultivated and preserved, its taste deepens and is enriched through proper care (right temperature, rotation, bottling, etc.). How much more do we need to nurture, protect, cultivate, and care for our precious children, whom God has entrusted to us.

Jesus Feeds His Children Physically:

"Then he took bread, said the blessing, broke it, and gave it to them, saying "This is my body" (Luke 22: 19). As mothers, we too feed our children physically – one meal at a time. Day by day, they mature and grow, moving toward adulthood and all that God has created them to be.

Jesus feeds His children Spiritually:

Often what happens in the physical world occurs in the spiritual realm. This was quite true at the Last Supper, as the food the disciples received became both the physical and spiritual body of Jesus.

While at my table, we will not experience a Eucharistic celebration, I can, however, (at times) provide opportunities for spiritual discussions through questions to ponder and debate. This allows for the sharing of our hearts, as we each talk about the highs and lows of our day. Further, this time of openness provides hope for the evening and the days to follow, as we unfold our dreams and plans. Most importantly, we have this special time to cover these hopes and challenges with prayer and encouragement. We discover, contemplate, and focus on where the Lord is moving in each of our lives.

Jesus Teaches His Children:

"He rose from supper and took off his outer garments. He took a towel and tied it around his waist. Then he poured water into a basin and began to wash the disciples' feet and dry them with a towel around his waist" (John 13: 4-5).

"Do you realize what I have done for you? You call me 'teacher and master,' and rightly so, for indeed I am. If I, therefore, the master and teacher, have washed your feet, you ought to wash one another's feet. I have given you a model to follow, so that as I have done for you, you should also do" (John13: 12b -15).

Jesus uses every opportunity to instruct His apostles, and this is most especially witnessed at the Last Supper. He gives His Apostles a model to follow and He gives clarity in direction.

As I meditate on this example, I can understand that I, too, may pass along instructions, priorities, and models around my table. My children can learn recipes, and graces, such as the art of setting a beautiful table. It does not take much planning to bring a poem, a photo, or a book to share after dinner. This type of sharing lends grace and significance to those special "things," both beautiful and treasured. And as the children grow older, it sets an example for them of steps and patterns to follow.

Jesus Speaks with Love to His Children:

"My children, I will be with you only a little while longer.... Love one another" (John 13: 33-34). Here we see Jesus speaking His Heart, declaring that the Apostles are in fact "His children" and gifting them with an extraordinary gift – the gift of a new commandment: to love one another.

In our family, at meals and shortly afterward, we sometimes take the time to communicate a sentiment or a new understanding. Children delight in (and need) to hear words of affirmation. In both the sharing and the responding, we all receive the gift of words.

Jesus Passes Along Responsibility:
"And I confer a kingdom on you, just as my Father has conferred one on me, so that you may eat and drink at my table in my kingdom; and you will sit on thrones judging the twelve tribes of Israel" (Luke 29-30).

Meal times are opportunities for blessings to be bestowed and gifts to be given. It is wise to use these occasions with intentionality and planning, as we pass on our family treasures. Most of these gems will not be physical in nature. We can impart memories, life lessons, thinking, and values. Indeed, it is not that we have just a little to share with our children, but that God has provided us with so many years "at table" with them, because we have so much to pass on – a rich family and spiritual inheritance.

Jesus Shares His Heart in Prayer:
Perhaps we most clearly see the Heart of Jesus as He prays and openly speaks to His Father: "I revealed your name to those whom you gave me out of the world. They belonged to you, and you gave them to me, and they have kept your word" (John 17:6).

Prayer is an expression of the heart. It carries words of faith and devotion. How wonderful it is for our children to hear us pray at meals. Whether it is a standard prayer or a more elaborate one, it carries our heart and our faith to our children. Our hearts BELIEVE in God and that God is GOOD. We are thankful.

I have also found that just as Jesus addressed His Father with simple heartfelt prayers, we, too, should pray meekly and sincerely with our children. While such sincerity makes us vulnerable, it allows us to convey so much of our parent heart to our children. Simple prayers, like "Lord, bless the cook who made this food"; "Lord we thank you for bringing a special friend to our table"; "Lord thank you for homemade barbeque sauce!" all convey our thankfulness and the expressions of our heart.

Jesus Highlights Unity:

"As I have loved you, so you also should love one another. This is how all will know that you are my disciples, if you have love for one another" (John 13: 34-35).

Consistent unity around the table will anchor us as a family through challenges and storms. Love builds. We want our family unity to be strong and remain constant. They receive the love with which we serve those around us, and they are able then to serve one another.

Eucharistic Miracles:

God is in the details, and He is most certainly in the details of the Eucharistic Miracles, which are a beautiful gift to the Church. Behind each one is a unique story – both human and holy – that leads to a miraculous move and revelation of the Lord. Every one of these miracles is worth uncovering and points us to the Lord and His ways – all are worth discovering and studying.

Several of these Eucharistic miracles involve the Eucharist physically appearing as the flesh and blood of Jesus. We see this in the Miracle of Orvieto (Italy) in 1263, and more recently in the grace and wonder of the miracle Buenos Aires that took place in the 1990s. After three years, the host, which had manifested living tissue, was scientifically examined. It was found to be living heart tissue with muscle cells and active white blood cells. The samples also indicated that the individual had suffered extreme duress.

How perfect that the Lord would choose to manifest His flesh in the Eucharist, and in the flesh of His Heart.

Dear homeschool Mother, the Eucharist is the source and summit of our faith and our center. The efforts we make to center our lives around this gift will help us learn and grow so that we and our children may be formed into the very Heart of Jesus, living Eucharists walking the earth.

God Bless,
Michelle

19: The Use of Technology

Dear Homeschooling Mom:

If there is one concern shared by most parents, I believe it is in the area of screen time – the unprecedented number of hours our kids spend on their devices, literally every day. Our hearts are for our children, specifically for their well-being, and this area of technology (both in and out of the academic setting) brings up many important questions.

Electronics – phones, tablets, computers – are not evil in and of themselves any more than a lamp or a desk is inherently bad. However, most parents agree that they are fearful of certain hidden (or obvious) dangers inherent in this new mode of teaching, learning, and communicating.

Obviously, we have been given tremendous tools. But I wonder if we have taken the time to consider why and how these connective devices can best be used. If we do not ask these questions, our supervision of our children in this area can be limited to "thou shall not," which provides little direction.

Example of Scouts

It can be helpful to look at all this from other perspectives. For example, Scouts are also given tools that they must learn how to safely use. In Scouting, before a child earns the right to carry a small knife, he/she must first learn the proper use of this handy, potentially destructive, tool. These young people are shown how a knife is appropriately used for cutting and carving. Through instruction, they come to understand that this versatile tool can be wielded to create beauty and yield practical results, all by cutting where needed and considering certain measurements and safety factors. Risks are emphasized with the idea of a "blood circle," meaning that this sharp instrument should not be employed when another person is within arm's length. It is to be used purposely, deliberately and in a focused manner – only when the Scout's full attention can be given to the tool at hand.

We need some similar controls when it comes to our connective devices. Just as we agree that a knife is used to cut and carve, we must identify and concentrate on how technology should best be used.

Technology is Powerful

Many of us have given our kids a smart phone with the understanding that in this day and age they "need it" for safety and security. While this may be true, we are giving them access to much more by placing in their hands such a powerful, all-encompassing tool. Like the scouting knife, a mobile phone can be used creatively and productively – or carelessly and destructively.

The Blessings of Technology

Connective devices effectively help us teach, learn, and communicate; they can be advantageous in so many ways! Below are just a few of the benefits and blessings.

Connection: With smart phones and tablets, we are able to interconnect quickly (and deeply) on matters that need to be communicated. We can even warn (or be notified) of impending threats. We are able to share suggestions and knowledge easily and instantly with others experiencing similar situations. This form of communication provides community, awareness, and a linking or joining of arms together.

Gathering: Connective devices are an extremely powerful gathering tool. Entire communities can be assembled in a matter of clicks. Events are able to be effectively planned and promoted; needs can be identified; requests are sent out for help. Our devices can amass large (or small) groups of individuals to be one in spirit, even while physically distant – whether on the other side of the globe or just around the corner.

Convenience: Being able to productively work from home or anywhere is advantageous in multiple ways. Computers are not only easily transportable, some come equipped with handy instruments and apps to bring order to our day – calendars, clocks, calculators, "to do" lists, maps, route planners, and so much more. Finally, there is the unprecedented wealth of knowledge "at our finger tips." We are functioning in an extraordinary time when every bit of available knowledge is easily accessible.

Community: Community can be initiated, built up, and nurtured through our devices. Encouraging words, sent by text, email, or social media enlivens hearts while inspiring images have the capacity to enkindle the flame of divine love. Technology can be a useful blessing, as we seek to know the Lord in a deeper and more abundant way.

The Dangers of Technology

Yet with all of the above blessings, these tools also come with certain fundamental risks:

A False Sense of Urgency: An unrealistic sense of immediacy can be falsely created in us, as we carry and use our devices. The lure of words and images on a screen too often takes us away from people, places, or projects that are more important. This can give rise to a habitual, though unintended, mixing up of priorities. I think we all have been there, deciding, "I need to answer that text or email," when in reality our response can wait. This impulsive response is often at the expense of time that could be invested in real life engagement with the people around us.

Distracted and Unavailable: Relationships are formed out of time spent together – sometimes quiet time and still time. Technology can distract from the forming of significant personal bonds and put relationships at risk. Friends and family can easily be wounded by another's seeming unavailability or lack of concern. Sometimes we ignore the loved one, friend, or new acquaintance there in front of us, unintentionally sending a message of indifference or rejection. Our personal devices become the priority, rather than our personal relationships. This is ironic, since the original intent of the technology was to make connectivity more possible.

Multi-Tasking: One of the greatest dangers I have observed, is the ease and appeal of multi-tasking. We are tempted to try to "do it all" pushing us beyond our own strength and capabilities. To be in a verbal conversation with two individuals at the same time is actually to be in no conversation with either of them. Our state highway laws have made it illegal to hold a phone while driving for this very reason. When done simultaneously, these tasks cannot (always) be done safely.

Unnatural "Depth" of Focus: Another danger is the total captivation that comes with screen time. I can easily put down a book I am reading when one of my children comes to me. But I have a much harder time turning my head from the screen. Screens are that much more engrossing and absorbing, thereby making us less aware of the people and activities around us. Minutes and hours simply slip by without our being aware of how much time we are devoting to devices. It is hard for us, even as adults, to exercise the discipline required to curb our screen time, and yet we expect our children to show this needed restraint and limit theirs.

Images and Exposure: The ease of access to harmful images and information is a very real and present danger to young hearts and minds. I have observed that the rabbit hole can open up in a split second, as one website quickly leads to another. Children are by nature curious – and we want them to be – but not on the computer. The pictures they see cannot be easily erased from their minds.

Emotional vs. Thoughtful Response: Technology allows fingers to fly on a keyboard, letting emotions overtake reason when expressing oneself, especially in the heat of the moment. Words can be hurtful, and teens are especially vulnerable to verbal barrages directed at them, even in a roundabout way. Language has meaning, and sadly for the one on the receiving end, misguided words can lead to fear, anxiety, obsession, depression, anger, and more.

Addiction: Finally, technology puts our minds in the mode of thinking one step ahead of the game as the brain excitedly anticipates the next click. Studies show that with each touch, a tiny amount of dopamine is released in the brain, thereby leading to addiction. This process literally takes the mind out of the present moment and into looking forward to the next "high," just a click away.

A Family Contract, Part of the Solution

A "family technology contract" might offer a partial solution to these problems. Such an agreement would be the goal of a family discussion of the positives and negatives of technology and the need for certain safeguards. Children succeed with direction and boundaries, especially in the era of electronics. I believe that we, as parents, should be the role models in this, the ones who first need to adhere to the family tech policies. The contracts are as much for us, as they are for our teens and younger children.

The discourse leading to the agreement should seek to identify and articulate the intended purpose of our use of technology, as well as the reasons for setting limits. Why is the connective device important at a certain time or in a particular setting? What do we hope to achieve through its use? How can we all be held accountable? And, obviously it is essential to re-evaluate these contracts, as life changes – both in terms of our academic and work pursuits and so-called upgrades or new purchases of different electronic devices.

Accountability Partner

Perhaps, due to the impulsivity factor that goes with screen use, most adults, not to mention teens, would do well to have an accountability partner. Just a weekly "check-in" would serve as a reminder of the contract and allow for encouragement and fresh starts. It is simply too easy to fall back into old habits. Knowing we will have a regular time of accountability goes a long way in helping us keep these commitments.

Focus on What the Technology is Accomplishing

To continue on this course with wisdom, it is good to set aside time to evaluate the outcomes we are seeing through the use of our technology. What activities have been made possible, what goals are being met, what communications have been enhanced? In short, is our technology being used for the purpose for which we intended it? Particularly during the customary school planning months – times such as August and January – it makes sense to give some thought to where technology is helping or hindering. That type of honest assessment will pave the way for more productive use of the tools we've been given, rather than allowing the tools to "use" us.

As we navigate these unchartered waters, we know that God walks with us and is giving us an extra measure of grace and help… we are so in need of both.

God Bless,
Michelle

20: Practical Tips

Dear Homeschooling Mom:

We all love practical tips... little pieces of advice that smooth over a bumpy road or a rough day. Just a bit of "tried and true" wisdom can form a bridge over "troubled waters," enabling one to continue on the journey.

To Be or Not to Be.... That is the Question

For so long my heart desired to answer the ever-present question, "What am I expected to do?" I yearned and prayed for quick discipline solutions, academic textbooks that would solve curriculum dilemmas, even techniques to instantaneously bring cleanliness and order to my house. These answers were not to be found, or at least they seemed in short supply. In prayer, I found that God was directing me more to the "person I was to be," than the plan(s) I was trying to set in motion. He was not calling me to be a computer or a robot. He desired that I learn to recognize His voice, to respond to His leading, and to direct others toward Him. And above all, He wanted me to let Him be God in every aspect of my life. All this was a challenging shift.

Once I found this path, it steadied my heart and allowed me to focus on what God really was asking of me in a given situation, which was often patience, perseverance, or trust. In this way, I was (and am) able to return to peace and let Him be my sovereign Lord. Turning circumstances and problems over to Him is vital, and doing so with transparency sets an example for my children.

Begin the Day with Prayer

For me, prayer begins my day in a beautiful way. Yes, it can feel like a sacrifice getting out of bed before my children – a really big sacrifice! But I have never regretted the time I've spent with the Lord. In fact, I wish I had more time to spend with Him listening to His voice.

Prayer is such a gift from God, and it lays a solid foundation for the day. This sacred, early morning time allows me to feel less "tackled" by the day's events, circumstances, and homeschool challenges. I am better able to respond to my children and various situations in a calm, positive, and forward looking manner.

Direct the Focus Toward the Higher Lessons

When a school teaching or life experience lends itself, I have found it very fulfilling to direct my children's attention toward the higher lessons. "Wow, God wanted you to see that butterfly on the yellow flower." Or, "What a loyal friend Sam (in Tolkien's *Lord of the Rings*) is to Frodo. Or, "only God could design such order in math." And in everything, "Christ's sacrifice was so perfect." By directing my children's thoughts heavenward, I am establishing a pattern for them to follow, creating a desire to gaze upon the world in a deeper, more beautiful way. It is also such a joy when "down the road" I hear my "voice" coming out of their mouths, as they behold a wonder of nature or reflect upon the writings of a particular author.

Slow and Steady Wins the Race

Consistency seems to me the best plan of attack in a myriad ways. Whether it's a first grader learning to read or a second grader learning his math facts, a smaller slice of a particular subject each day (ultimately) proves more fruitful than a full hour of combined sequential lessons. A simple first-grade schedule, for example, that devotes fifteen minutes each to math and phonics, followed by a brief period of reading aloud, can lead to impressive results. I have been amazed at the learning that takes place through just a small investment in those two key subjects – reading and math. It almost seems miraculous how such small seeds of teaching and learning (with regular watering) grow and thrive, yielding an amazing homeschool harvest. This slow steady pace can be counted on for consistent growth.

Beware of Excessive Creativity in Lesson Planning

A veteran homeschool mom shared with me many years ago that creativity in lesson planning, with all its usefulness, can also be exhausting. She relayed a true story about two mothers wading through their first year of homeschooling. The first did simple lesson planning: she used a typical straightforward math curriculum, a science textbook, and a widely recommended history program. The other decided to bring life and enrichment to her homeschool through historical reenactments, numerous science experiments, a complex use of math manipulatives, and more. The first was still homeschooling ten years later and undoubtedly had grown and added curriculum components in measured ways. And the second? She called it quits after the first year – she was simply too worn out!

Have "Homeschool Time" and Stick to the Plan

It can be tempting, very tempting (knowing that you have the whole day to homeschool) to get sidetracked – to perhaps talk to a friend or go for a walk. Personally, I have found that it works best to have a set time for homeschool each day and stick with the schedule. Our own homeschool hours generally run from 10:00 am to 2:00 pm with designated segments for some independent work in the afternoon. During these hours, I turn off the cell phone and use the computer only for teaching purposes, as I try to be fully present and engaged as a mother and teacher.

Consider Six to Eight Week Stretches

It invariably happens every year. I dive in and excitedly open new books and pursue fresh plans. Then, about two weeks into the new school year, I decide that one piece of the curriculum I've chosen is simply not working. I am tempted to begin looking for replacement materials to insert. However, I've found that a better path is to continue on the journey with the selected program for six to eight weeks. Wait for a break, and then reassess. If different learning tools are still needed, I can now make decisions with the knowledge of what's been tried and found lacking.

Six to eight week stretches, followed by a week's break, also allows for homeschooling moms to take a breather and catch up on the details of life, such as ever-present home organizing. Quite simply, we need to rest from schooling for a bit. These breaks are also the perfect time to reevaluate what is or is not working. And we can make necessary changes and reenter the "classroom" from a place of rest and refreshment.

Do Not Make Any Changes in February

In February, the earth is cold, trees are bare, and we may personally feel tired and worn. It seems to me that this is the time of year when some homeschool moms are looking at the yellow bus passing their street and thinking, "Hmm, it might be nice…." At the same time, some moms with their children in school are observing homeschool families and thinking to themselves, "Maybe it's time to consider a different approach to learning for my kids."

Decisions this big and life-changing are best made in the spring. May, when the earth is blooming with new life, is a good time. Then, one can see all the fruits of her labor from the school year, now ending. We can better evaluate the past nine months, in this season of promise, than when the ground is still cold and hard!

Go with Gentleness

We have the best dentist in the whole world. She is so gentle, in fact, that much of the time, I almost forget she is working on my teeth – and the mouth is one of the most sensitive parts of the body. I have observed the technique she uses when she works on a sensitive spot. This gentle dentist works just a bit on the problem area, then moves on, before returning momentarily to the sensitive area. She continues in this back-and-forth manner, making progress at a steady pace, while I am barely aware of the procedure being performed.

I'm certainly not comparing our children's homeschool experience with a trip to the dentist! However, if certain subjects are more challenging because it's not your child's inclination or strong suit, and they are trying to avoid this academic area, consider smaller doses interspersed with more satisfying, even joyful pursuits.

Consider What the Lesson Really Is

What God is doing is far more important than any plan or schedule. Although math needs to be taught, when a crying baby awakes it is important to tend to the infant, thereby allowing the children to see this display of docile and maternal love. The lesson we are intent on teaching may not be what the Lord is teaching at the moment. It is very important to ask the question during these times, "What is

God doing and what does He 'will' for me to do at this point in time?" Often, the answer is not math.

Cultivate a Love of Children

Motherhood was a real adjustment for me, and sometimes it feels like I'm still adjusting! I don't have it all figured out, and I continue to grow. Yet, the blessings are beyond measure. While growing up, my brother and I were fairly close in age, so I did not have the experience (like some older sisters) of caring for younger siblings. When I was older, I babysat for other families on occasion. College propelled me into a business mindset, and marriage provided such welcome warmth. Imagine my "horror" when I discovered my six-week-old did not want to sleep in on Saturdays! Motherhood was a tremendous adjustment for me! Even today, I have to admit that at times it is still a daily struggle for me to lay down my life, to do what is best for my children.

Yes, my children have been the most tremendous blessing to me. They have taught me joy and wonder. They have taught me to slow down and to live in the present moment. They have taught me not to be afraid. From them I have learned to go with the flow, to enjoy the process of watching and waiting, and being part of their unfolding. They have taught me humility. They have given me the gift of being on my knees to kiss a boo-boo or to teach a lesson one more time. Most of all, they have inspired me to seek and find Jesus Christ. I am so rewarded by their joy, their wonder, their hearts.

Thirty Seconds Each Day

I have always found it a bit humorous when experienced mothers tell a new mom, "just enjoy your baby." The new mother is sleep deprived, struggling to even think in complete sentences, learning how to manage a very different household and a baby, not to mention fighting through thoughts of what she should be doing or not doing. Despite all that, she is just "supposed to enjoy the baby"? Alas, sometimes we're not sure what that means.

Eventually, we transition to total enjoyment of our new infant, spending time totally fixated on their every smile and gesture. I encourage you to find similar joy in this same child, at every age and stage. Take some time each day to look at your child for thirty seconds. Take in the beauty, the awe, the wonder, the joy of the presence of God alive and well, right before your eyes.

Be still and silent before this presence of God in your midst. Look for and thank God for the smile, the wonder, the quirks, the humor, the funny expressions, the habits, the personality, the growth, and the heart of this particular child. Thirty seconds. You are passing along a tremendous gift to your young one or teen in doing this. Not only will they feel "warm and fuzzy" and loved, but hopefully they, too, will one day look and "adore" the Jesus in their own child(ren) some twenty years down the road.

Don't Compare the Inside of Your Homeschool to the Outside of Someone Else's

Every homeschool mother struggles with children, schedules, activities, and balance. What may look like tasks, accomplished with ease, is most likely just as difficult and messy in "the other mother's" home as it is in yours. Have no doubt, they have their clutter and chaos, too.

Don't Expect to Have a Clean House All the Time

With children living underfoot – and "doing life" all the time, it is still tempting to think that a clean house can be maintained throughout the day or week, while still homeschooling. After sixteen years in this role and lifestyle, I can count on perhaps one hand the homeschool mothers I've encountered who keep an entire clean house, as in every room and nook and cranny, all at once.

I've found a daily cleaning schedule to be a more realistic approach: floors on Fridays, bathrooms on Saturdays, maybe deep cleaning one or two rooms each week, and/or picking up toys at the end of the night. Not having an unrealistic expectation seems to cultivate a bit of peace and routine. (No, this is not a book about cleaning, but homeschooling does take place at home, so "domestic order" is part of the challenge!)

A Few Extra Tips – Fines and Wines
Quote of the Day

I once jokingly said to a friend that most homeschooling mothers' problems can be solved either by a cup of coffee or a glass of wine. That's obviously not true, but we do sometimes need a coffee break, an afternoon cup of tea, a glass of wine in the evening with our husband, or whatever relaxes us – perhaps a hot bath!

(The practical tip is: don't forget the little pick-me-ups – they can work wonders!)

Don't Worry about Library Fines

We visit the library often and read lots and lots of books. It happens regularly that I return books a day or a week late, and as a result incur a fine. I have made peace with these charges. The joy and wisdom the children glean from the library books far outweigh any fine! I would rather go to the library and gather a basket of books, than forego this "free" educational resource, out of fear of having to pay a fine.

Always Turn to Jesus

One evening, after a trying day with one of my "munchkins" (who had been especially wiggly that day), I "escaped" and went to Eucharistic Adoration to be with Jesus alone.

Jesus was so tangibly present, as I knelt before Him. My heart wanted my wiggly munchkin to be with Jesus. And so*, in my mind*, I brought my child to church. As the day had been trying, I felt my child needed to be closer to Jesus. Again, *in my mind*, I shrunk him and placed him on the altar next to Jesus in the monstrance. But still this was not close enough. So once more, I shrunk my child even smaller, and *in my mind* opened the monstrance and popped this wiggly child inside the monstrance, closed it, and walked out of church leaving my precious child with Jesus. Jesus had him – wiggles and all.

I have found that recalling and meditating on this image and trusting Jesus with a child, a situation, or a problem allows Him to give the grace needed – either to the child or to me. He has it.

I am praying that these fresh tips may help you successfully cross a bridge or navigate a bump, as you journey along the road of homeschooling.

God Bless,
Michelle

Appendix

Prayer for the Abode of God
by Michelle Heekin

Almighty God and Father, I give you this place we call home, where the walls bless our family with a place to dwell and live together. *We pray our home may be given extraordinary graces and blessing.*

In heaven, You are revered as God and Father, and heaven is Your home. *May our Blessed Mother obtain for us the grace to make this dwelling a home, a little "mercy seat" or footstool where You are pleased to dwell even resting "your feet" as Father among Your children.*

In heaven, Your name is reverenced as Holy, You are honored with praises and thanksgivings. *May our Blessed Mother obtain for us the grace to be united to the praises of the angels and the saints proclaiming You as Holy, Holy, Holy.*

In heaven, Your will is accomplished at every moment and the words "Your kingdom come, Your will be done" are fulfilled. *May our Blessed Mother obtain for us the grace to be united to You in accomplishing Your work fulfilling the words "on earth as it is in heaven".*

In heaven, Your angels stand guard, and You protect, guard, and govern all that You have created. *May our Blessed Mother obtain for us the grace to be united with Your abode in heaven, a strong fortress, where only goodness, and holiness dwell.*

In heaven, Your works are accomplished, and there is no limit to the length of Your arm, the strength of Your power, and the magnitude of Your works. *May our Blessed Mother obtain for us the grace to be united in Your redemptive work of salvation. May You accomplish great works within the walls of our home.*

In heaven, You all dwell in unity of spirit as Jesus prayed the words "our Father." *May the Blessed Mother obtain for us the grace to be united in the spirit, so that harmony, and peace may reign here.*

In heaven, You choose to dwell among the angels and the saints. *May our Blessed Mother obtain for us the grace to have many angels and saints present in our midst.*

Mother Mary pray for us, that we may dwell with God our heavenly Father.
AMEN

LITANY OF TRUST
by The Sisters of Life

From the belief that I have to earn Your love
Deliver me, Jesus.
From the fear that I am unlovable
Deliver me, Jesus.
From the false security that I have what it takes
Deliver me, Jesus.
From the fear that trusting You will leave me more destitute
Deliver me, Jesus.
From all suspicion of Your words and promises
Deliver me, Jesus.
From the rebellion against childlike dependency on You
Deliver me, Jesus.
From refusals and reluctances in accepting Your will
Deliver me, Jesus.
From anxiety about the future
Deliver me, Jesus.
From resentment or excessive preoccupation with the past
Deliver me, Jesus.
From restless self-seeking in the present moment
Deliver me, Jesus.
From disbelief in Your love and presence
Deliver me, Jesus.
From the fear of being asked to give more than I have
Deliver me, Jesus.
From the belief that my life has no meaning or worth
Deliver me, Jesus.
From the fear of what love demands
Deliver me, Jesus.
From discouragement
Deliver me, Jesus.

That You are continually holding me, sustaining me, loving me
Jesus, I trust in You.
That Your love goes deeper than my sins and failings and transforms me
Jesus, I trust in You.
That not knowing what tomorrow brings is an invitation to lean on You
Jesus, I trust in You.
That You are with me in my suffering
Jesus, I trust in You.
That my suffering, united to Your own, will bear fruit in this life and the next
Jesus, I trust in You.
That You will not leave me orphan, that You are present in Your Church
Jesus, I trust in You.
That Your plan is better than anything else
Jesus, I trust in You.
That You always hear me and in Your goodness always respond to me
Jesus, I trust in You.
That You give me the grace to accept forgiveness and to forgive others
Jesus, I trust in You.
That You give me all the strength I need for what is asked
Jesus, I trust in You.
That my life is a gift
Jesus, I trust in You.
That You will teach me to trust You
Jesus, I trust in You.
That You are my Lord and my God
Jesus, I trust in You.
That I am Your beloved one
Jesus, I trust in You.

Prayer of Faith and Hope
by Michelle Heekin

I believe that You, my Almighty Father hold all things in Your Sovereign hands.

Father, I pray, Your kingdom come and Your will be done.

I believe that Your love works all things together for good and even for the greatest good for those who love You.

Father, I pray, Your Kingdom come and Your will be done.

I believe in the depth of Your love for me. Any challenging situation I encounter only more deeply confirms Your love for me as You place Your trust in me.

Father, I pray, Your Kingdom come and Your will be done.

I believe the more challenging the struggle I face, the taller I am asked to grow in trust, faith and holiness; a tall pillar upon which the Church can find support.

Father, I pray, Your kingdom come and Your will be done.

I believe Your infinite knowledge far surpasses my limited sight. You behold the present, together with the past and future. You see in a completed tapestry what I see in a tiny thread.

Father, I pray, Your kingdom come and Your will be done.

I believe in Your infinite wisdom. You often will my silence and stillness in many challenging situations; which allows You to act in Your perfect timing and in Your perfect way.

Father, I pray, Your kingdom come and Your will be done.

I believe if/when you will that I step forward in faith You will illuminate my steps with clarity and set before me a path of peace and righteousness.

Father, I pray, Your kingdom come and Your will be done.

I believe You have willed this season of patient waiting and expectation as a time to deepen my Hope in Your promises and as a time of dwelling upon the "things that are above."

Father, I pray, Your kingdom come and Your will be done.

I believe I am especially blessed during this time to be more deeply united in the praises of the angels and saints. Any pain or suffering will not distract me from rejoicing in the merits and victory of Jesus, Your beloved Son and my Savior.

Father, I pray, Your kingdom come and Your will be done.

I believe Your Fatherly Heart understands my brokenness, broken heartedness and suffering. Your Heart is pierced by any wounds I bear. Compassion and tenderness are in Your hands as they lead, guide and heal me.

Father, I pray, Your kingdom come and Your will be done.

I believe in choosing to unite my suffering to Your Son's, any burden I carry can bear the fruit of patience, kindness, gentleness, and faithfulness; and serve as a prayer for the conversion of others. This trial is only for a season to be followed by a glorious springtime of conversion. The burial slab of Jesus was the first stone to see the resurrection.

Father, I pray, Your kingdom come and Your will be done.

I believe in the grace of today which I accept as a gift from You. I believe that You desire I live today in fullness of joy, peace, faith and hope.

Father, I pray, Your kingdom come, Your will be done.

Amen

Children are not a distraction from more important work. They are the MOST important work.
C.S. Lewis

ABOUT THE AUTHOR

Michelle Heekin lives in Georgia with her "saint Joseph" of 25 years and four children. She has homeschooled for 17 years with various settings and curriculums. She has a master's degree in Social Work from the University of Alabama, a bachelor's degree from Saint Mary's College, and has also studied abroad in Rome. Before becoming a mom and beginning her homeschool journey, she worked for Catholic Social Services with birth-mothers who made the decision to continue their pregnancy, preparing them to parent or place their child with an adoptive family. She has been a member of the Catholic Charismatic Movement for 35 years and has organized numerous retreats and evenings of reflection. In her spare time, she can be found in the garden, cuddled up reading a book, gathered with family and friends, or taking a nap.

She can be contacted at michelleheekin@gmail.com

Michelle Heekin

Made in USA - Crawfordsville, IN
48002_9780578973968
09.27.2021 0515